EXPOSING
SPIRITUAL ABUSE

MIKE FEHLAUER

EXPOSING
SPIRITUAL ABUSE

Charisma®
HOUSE
Books about Spirit-Led Living

EXPOSING SPIRITUAL ABUSE by Mike Fehlauer
Published by Charisma House
A part of Strang Communications Company
600 Rinehart Road
Lake Mary, Florida 32746
www.charismahouse.com

Unless otherwise noted, all Scripture quotations are from the
New King James Version of the Bible. Copyright © 1979, 1980,
1982 by Thomas Nelson, Inc., publishers. Used by permission.

Scripture quotations marked AMP are from the Amplified Bible.
Old Testament copyright © 1965, 1987 by the Zondervan
Corporation. The Amplified New Testament copyright © 1954,
1958, 1987 by the Lockman Foundation. Used by permission.

Scripture quotations marked KJV are from the King James
Version of the Bible.

Scripture quotations marked NAS are from the New American
Standard Bible. Copyright © 1960, 1962, 1963, 1968, 1971,
1972, 1973, 1975, 1977 by the Lockman Foundation.
Used by permission. (www.Lockman.org)

Scripture quotations marked AMP are from the Amplified Bible.
Old Testament copyright © 1965, 1987 by the Zondervan
Corporation. The Amplified New Testament copyright © 1954,
1958, 1987 by the Lockman Foundation. Used by permission.

Cover design by Brenda Haun

Library of Congress Catalog Card Number: 2001092759
International Standard Book Number: 0-88419-768-9

Incidents and persons portrayed in this book are based
on fact. Some names, places and other identifying details
may have been changed and altered to protect the privacy
and anonymity of the individuals to whom they refer. Any
similarity between the names and stories of individuals
known to readers is coincidental and not intentional.

01 02 03 04 05   8 7 6 5 4 3 2 1
Printed in the United States of America

CONTENTS

CHAPTER 1

IS THE EMPEROR REALLY NAKED?

"If anyone dares to ask a question about how the money is used, the pastor accuses him of being distrustful or disobedient," Steve explained. And for the last three years, he added, the pastor's sermons almost always focused on the topic of submission to spiritual authority. "If anyone leaves the church," Steve told Mark, "the pastors label him *rebellious,* or they tell us he was offended."

Mark heard a familiar voice on the other end of the line when he answered the phone late one evening: "Mark, can we talk? I'm really concerned that our church is becoming…well, it's almost…a cult."

Mark hadn't heard from his friend Steve in three years. They both had attended the same Charismatic church until Mark's career required him to relocate to another state. Consequently they had lost touch with each other. Now, in desperation, Steve was reaching out to someone outside his close-knit world.

It was clear that Steve's apprehension was the result of personal observations and not just based on church gossip. Up to this point Steve had been careful not to discuss his thoughts with anyone. He was actually afraid to talk about the subject. Steve was particularly bothered by an attitude of secrecy concerning the church's finances.

"If anyone dares to ask a question about how the money is used, the pastor accuses him of being distrustful or disobedient," Steve explained. And for the last three years, he added, the pastor's sermons almost always focused on the topic of submission to spiritual authority. "If anyone leaves the church," Steve told Mark, "the pastors label him *rebellious*, or they tell us he was offended."

3

Mark grew more concerned as Steve nervously shared more details. "The pastor also told us that since God brought us to the church, he, as the pastor, is our spiritual father, and we should never leave unless God tells him first," Steve said. "He even told us that if we ever left without pastoral permission, we would be vulnerable to Satan's destruction."

When their conversation ended, Mark realized that

his friend was trapped in an extremely unhealthy spiritual situation. He urged his friend to set up an appointment with the pastor in order to confront him about his concerns. "You can't subject yourself or your family to that kind of control, Steve," Mark advised.

A week later, Mark talked with Steve again and discovered just how strong the pastor's influence was over this congregation. Steve had apologized to the pastor for talking with an outsider about his problems with the church, and he pledged that he would never talk with Mark again.

Mark has not heard from Steve since.

The scenario I just described is a true story—and it is much more typical than any of us would like to admit. The sad truth is that many churches today struggle with varying degrees of control, which can lead to devastating abuse if not corrected. That abuse has resulted in untold thousands of wounded and disillusioned Christians who believe they've been burned by the one institution in the world that was supposed to help them.

I am sure that almost everyone would admit there are instances of spiritual abuse in the church. But how prevalent are these situations? I think the current thought has been that any situation of abuse is so rare that it doesn't need to be addressed—and certainly not confronted. Many believe there are far greater problems confronting the church than the abuse by controlling preachers toward parishioners.

For example, time and time again I have heard preachers complain that the biggest problem facing the church is not abuse by the clergy, but the rebellion of the people to authority. Therefore, they surmise, a

4

book on spiritual abuse is not only unnecessary, but also it doesn't address the "real" problem. Some have gone so far as say that such a book will only ignite more rebellion within the church.

How Big Is the Problem?

In February 1999, I wrote an article for *Charisma* magazine titled "Five Warning Signs of an Unhealthy

> # He urged his friend to set up an appointment with the pastor in order to confront him about his concerns.

Church." The article created a maelstrom of response. Many of the letters were from pastors who vocalized their fear that this article would only serve to increase the problem of rebellion in the church.

One pastor from the state of Washington wrote:

5

> I am extremely disappointed in *Charisma* and its editors for printing Mike Fehlauer's article on controlling churches. If you haven't noticed, there is a spirit of rebellion that is loosed in our society and has spread into the church. There is a growing insistence on "rights" that has been distorted to justify rebellion and disobedience.
>
> The time is long overdue for pastors to courageously but lovingly stand up to lead and feed the flock. We do not need leaders who cave in to the fear of appearing controlling because they correct or direct their flocks...

This pastor continued by writing:

> Your article gives permission for any member to leave a church because of any correction a pastor might give. As soon as the recipient doesn't like the correction (and they seldom do), they scream "control," and seek to influence others, then run themselves.[1]

Another pastor from Canada expressed his displeasure, saying:

> *Charisma* has done a significant disservice to every local church with Mike Fehlauer's article on unhealthy churches. By failing to explain proper, biblical submission to spiritual authority, you have nurtured the seeds of suspicion and mistrust that are rampant in the church today. Important issues about pastoral oversight were referred to ambiguously or were placed within a context of extreme situations—making the appropriate use of pastoral authority almost taboo.
>
> For example, Fehlauer mentions that "controlling spiritual leaders insist upon 'pastoral permission' for someone to leave a church or relocate." Yet there are proper biblical grounds for people to seek counsel about such major life decisions.
>
> Often when people want to relocate, they are just chasing money rather than the will of God and don't want to speak with those in spiritual authority. Pastors have a responsibility to their congregations to help them understand that just because someone says that God told them to do something doesn't mean He did...[2]

6

As a result of the views represented in these letters, many leaders in the church have condemned the people of God for being rebellious, stiff-necked and uncommitted to the gospel. I agree that there are far too many who fit this description. Yet, in the New

Abuse has resulted in untold thousands of wounded and disillusioned Christians who believe they've been burned by the one institution in the world that was supposed to help them.

Testament, the ultimate responsibility for the state of the church isn't laid at the feet of the people, but rather at the feet of the pastors.

7

On those occasions in the Scriptures when Jesus speaks harshly, He is not speaking to sinners—He is speaking to *religious leaders*. It was the preachers of His day who were using their spiritual positions to take advantage of the people who caused Jesus to become angry. In Matthew 23:27 Jesus says, "Woe to you, scribes and Pharisees, hypocrites! For you are like whitewashed tombs which indeed appear beautiful outwardly, but inside are full of dead men's bones and all uncleanness." In Mark 12:38–40 Jesus adds, "Beware of the scribes, who desire to go around in long robes, love greetings in the marketplaces, the best seats in the synagogues, and the best places at feasts, who devour widows' houses, and for a pretense [or, appearance's sake] make long prayers. These will receive greater condemnation."

The ultimate responsibility for the state of the church isn't laid at the feet of the people, but rather at the feet of the pastors.

Why is it possible for religious leaders to receive a greater condemnation? Why, in James 3:1, do we read, "My brethren, let not many of you become teachers, knowing that we shall receive a stricter judgment"? It is because those who lead have the power to bring God's people, as sheep, into green pastures—or to lead them to desert places.

As leaders, we can't afford to assume that those we are called to serve are not interested in responding to God's Word. We can't afford to identify those to whom we are ministering as "problems." In truth, ultimately people respond to leadership—positively or negatively. In the Scriptures, people are referred to as sheep—not because sheep are considered some of the dumbest animals on earth, but because sheep require a shepherd.

There is a popular children's story that illustrates perfectly the approach we have had concerning spiritual abuse in the church. It is the story titled "The Emperor's New Clothes." The story is long, so I'll paraphrase it.

As the story goes, many years ago there lived an

8

emperor who was so fond of new clothes that he spent all his money on expensive garments. He wasn't concerned if his soldiers were taken care of. He wasn't interested in fulfilling his responsibilities as a ruler. All he really cared about was showing off his new clothes. He even had a coat for every hour of the day.

Two con men visited the emperor, representing themselves as weavers. By playing upon the emperor's arrogance, these thieves convinced the emperor that, for a price, they could weave him clothes from the finest silk. The silk was so fine, as a matter of fact, and the strands so thin that only the wisest and most loyal servants would be able to see his beautiful new garments.

These two rogues proceeded to sit at empty looms, pretending to weave a new suit for the emperor. Then the two crooks pretended to place the new suit on the emperor. The emperor's servants, not wanting to be labeled stupid or unfit for service, all commented on how beautiful the emperor's new suit was.

The emperor planned a processional through the streets of the city to show off his new suit. As he walked naked through the streets, no one wanted to appear to be stupid, so they all complimented the emperor on his clothes. The emperor himself did not want to admit that he was naked. Finally, a child called out, "The emperor is naked!"

Interestingly, it wasn't until a child broke the silence, calling out that the emperor wore no suit, that the other townspeople began to admit to the emperor's nakedness. Still too proud to admit his nakedness, the emperor decided that his best response was to lift his head in pride and continue to march through the city as if there were nothing wrong.

I don't know a story that better illustrates the

9

approach we have taken concerning the subject of spiritual abuse. The emperor wasn't willing to confront the truth of his nakedness. The truth meant he had to admit he was wrong. It required facing up to

Those who lead have the power to bring God's people, as sheep, into green pastures—or to lead them to desert places.

the fact he *had been* deceived—indeed, more importantly, that he could be deceived. The truth required a vulnerability that his insecurity wouldn't allow him to accept. It was pride that drew the emperor into his deception—the same pride that wouldn't allow him to admit his obvious weakness and insecurity. The emperor was more concerned about keeping up appearances than he was about the truth.

10

NAKED EMPERORS TODAY

Just as the emperor was too proud to admit his own nudity, leaders today throughout the body of Christ have been too proud to recognize their own spiritual nakedness. Just as the emperor was deceived by two thieves into thinking that he was wearing a beautiful suit, many pastors and preachers have been deceived by Satan into thinking they are clothed in God's power. Far too many leaders in the body of Christ are parading themselves through the streets under the illusion they are clothed in God's authority when, in reality, they have nothing on! They are walking in their own authority—not God's.

When you are walking in God's authority, you don't have to declare it. Those who walk in God's authority don't have to demand loyalty and obedience. God's power doesn't *demand*—it *leads*. God's authority doesn't *destroy*—it *brings hope and healing*. God's authority isn't based in insecurity; therefore, it has no need to control or manipulate.

Is Spiritual Abuse Really a Problem?

The *Charisma* magazine article "Five Warning Signs of an Unhealthy Church" was one of the most-responded-to articles ever published in the magazine. The editor was inundated with responses—from laity and preachers alike. Many of the responses were printed in the "Letters" page, yet there were too many responses to print all of them.

The amount of response indicates that the problem of spiritual abuse is far from rare. It is obvious that it is rampant and more widespread than we have wanted to believe. I am well aware that there are those who claim they have suffered abuse when no actual abuse has ever taken place. I will be dealing with this dynamic in a later chapter. Yet, more and more, we are discovering examples of the abuse of spiritual power within the church.

"A matter of loyalty"

One such example of abuse took place in a small Midwestern town. Sally had been a member of her church for years. Many times over the years she had noticed signs of unhealthy control, but each time she pushed her concerns aside, convincing herself that she

11

didn't have the right to question her pastor—not even in her own mind.

In addition, because of the abuse she had experienced as a child, Sally had struggled with fear for most of her life. Sometimes without warning she would find herself arrested with paralyzing panic attacks.

One day Ann, a friend of Sally's, shared with her about a time of renewal that was happening in a neighboring church. Several miraculous healings had taken place during the special services. Ann called Sally and told her what God was doing. Sally was excited and wanted to attend the renewal services to receive prayer for deliverance, and Sally and Ann decided to ride to the service together.

When Ann showed up that evening, Sally came out to greet her. As Ann approached the house, she saw Sally standing on her porch quietly crying. A pained expression was evident on Sally's face. "Sally, what's wrong?" Ann asked.

Sally just looked at her friend.

"Are you still going with me to church?" Ann asked.

"I shouldn't go."

"Why?"

Sally didn't respond, but just continued to stare. Remembering the times in the past when she had witnessed the control that Sally's pastor had over her, Ann asked, "Did your pastor say you couldn't go?"

Slowly Sally nodded her head.

"Sally," Ann exclaimed, "it's just another church service. And it's even on a night when your church has no regular services."

With an almost apologetic expression, Sally shrugged her shoulders, quickly turned and disappeared through the front door.

Later, Ann learned that Sally's pastor had heard she was planning to attend the service that night. He had called, offering the explanation that whatever Sally

They are walking in their own authority—not God's.

needed spiritually she would find in her church— under his leadership. The pastor made it clear that this was a matter of loyalty. Even though it wasn't verbalized, it was understood that if she wanted to continue to experience God's blessing—and his—she should not attend the service that night. Even though Sally's husband had encouraged her to go, Sally felt that she needed to submit to her pastor's authority by obeying his words.

"YOU ARE NOT READY YET"

In another situation, a traveling preacher asked a young lady to provide special music at a service he was conducting in a local church in the same city as her home church. When the preacher extended the invitation, he asked her if providing special music at his meeting would interfere with any responsibilities she had at her church. She was one of the singers in the worship team at her church. Because there were several singers on the team, they were scheduled on a rotation basis. She rarely missed a service, and never missed one in order to minister somewhere else. Therefore, since she wasn't scheduled to sing at her own church, she consented to sing at the neighboring church.

When her pastor found out about it, he called her into his office and scolded her for singing at the other

13

church. He said that it was wrong for her to take her anointing out of her home church.

By leaving and going to another church, where she had another pastor, she would become a spiritual "adulteress."

Later, this same young lady had an opportunity to travel full time as a vocalist with a well-known song evangelist—something she had always wanted to do. When she counseled with her pastor about it, she was told that "she wasn't ready." "And," her pastor continued, "I'll let you know when you are ready."

After several years of faithful service in the worship department of her local church, she is still waiting for her pastor to tell her when she is ready to fulfill her call in music ministry. (Here's an interesting side note to this story—in almost twenty years of existence, there has not been a single instance when any individual was told he or she was "ready" to leave the church to fulfill a ministry call.)

"It's spiritual adultery"

Because of the heavy-handed control that increased over the years in another church, one couple decided to attend a different church. They had stayed for years, hoping that things would get better. But when the control and manipulation outweighed the positive impact they were able to receive from the pastor's

14

messages, they decided to leave. Before they did, they phoned their pastor. First they thanked him for his contribution in their lives over the years. Then they explained their position as well as informed him of their decision to leave.

A few days later, the wife was visited by the wife of a staff member of the church. This staff member's wife told the woman that by leaving the church she was committing "spiritual adultery." Why? Because she was married to the church and therefore spiritually married to the pastor. By leaving and going to another church, where she had another pastor, she would become a spiritual "adulteress." The staff member's wife told her that unless she repented and returned to the church, she and her husband could never expect the blessings of God in their lives.

Another lady e-mailed me about the church she and her husband attend, where they have seen control directed toward others—and have experienced it personally as well. She had concluded that the whole purpose of the church was to teach the people to serve the pastor. For example, the courses in their church Bible school included:

15

- Serving the Man of God
- Being an Armor Bearer to the Man of God
- Qualifying for the Double Portion by Serving
- Your Pastor As Your Spiritual Father
- Giving Yourself to Your Pastor's Vision
- Honoring the Man of God

She went on to write:

> Without going into detail, there is much control

and manipulation. The leadership have made some in the church "pets" who are their informants in the body. People are played against each other. Many have left the church. For the past three or four months I have been scheduling my twelve-hour shifts on church days so that I have an excuse not to be there.

At first I totally believed everything the pastor preached and would have given all up for the "vision." I spent many hours at the church serving in his tape ministry. I resigned from doing the tapes in August. I left detailed information for my replacement so his tape ministry could continue to run smoothly.

I never made a good "yes" man, and sparks flew often once I realized what was going on. I didn't "fall in line." Recently, the pastor sent me a pot of flowers with a card saying "Missing you. Pastor So-and-so." Why? I don't know.

This lady's e-mail continued to express her hurt and confusion over what she should do next.

16

The "Five-Seven-Nine" rule

Here is another shocking example that took place in a church in the not-too-distant past. After serving for several years in the children's department of a large church, Cathy decided that she needed a break from children's ministry. She wanted to experience the services in the main sanctuary. One Sunday, Cathy noticed that the worship team was looking for singers. She had studied music, had a wonderful voice and loved to sing. She saw this as an opportunity to be involved and contribute to the worship experience in the adult service. She filled out the application and anxiously waited to hear from the music director.

Cathy's husband happened to have lunch with the music director shortly afterward. In the course of their lunch the music director brought up Cathy's application. Then he added, "I just wanted you to know that I didn't submit her application. She's too fat to be one of the praise singers."

Cathy's husband was stunned. It took him a while to regain his composure. He asked the music director to repeat what he had said. *Surely I misunderstood,* he thought. But the music director repeated what he had said, seemingly oblivious to the inappropriateness of his statement.

Cathy's husband asked the director, "What if Sandi Patti began to attend the church and wanted to be one of the praise singers? Would you let her be on the praise team?" The music director had no answer.

Cathy's husband later discovered that they actually had a policy to weed out overweight applicants. It was called the "Five-Seven-Nine" rule. A woman who wanted to be a praise singer had to be able to wear a size five, seven or nine dress. Cathy's husband approached the pastor of the church concerning this policy. The pastor said that he wasn't aware of such a policy. But later on, Cathy's husband received a phone call from one of the elders. The elder rebuked Cathy's husband for complaining about the policy. He was told by the elder that by bringing up the policy he was in rebellion to spiritual authority. Even if the policy was insulting and insensitive, his responsibility was to submit and not cause any problems. Cathy's husband replied by saying that if they were going to have that policy for woman on the platform, they should have the same policy for the men, even the pastors—who were all overweight.

17

"YOU ARE IN REBELLION"

In a book titled *The Subtle Power of Spiritual Abuse*, authors David Johnson and Jeff VanVonderen include the following example of manipulation and abuse:[3]

> Jeri sat in the office of a Christian counselor, explaining that she felt desperate, and felt like she was going crazy. "Either that," she said dryly, "or I'm on the verge of a major breakthrough in my spiritual growth."
>
> "Those are two big opposites," the counselor noted. "How did you come to that conclusion?"
>
> "Well," she began, choking up, "I went to my pastor a few months ago because I was feeling depressed a lot. He pegged the root problem right away, but I can't seem to do anything about it."
>
> "Root problem..." the counselor repeated. "What was that?"
>
> Jeri looked down at her shoe tops. "I guess I would have to say the problem is, well, me. My pastor says I'm in rebellion against God."

18

What unfolded was an unfortunate and all-too-common case history: Jeri's church teaches that Scripture is God's Word, the standard by which we must live. But they use it as a measure by which we gain acceptance with God rather than as a guide for living. Therefore, when she asked her pastor for help with her depression, she was given a "prescription" of praise Scriptures to memorize and repeat over and over. This, she was told, would get her mind off herself and onto God. The depression would lift when she got over her sinful self-centeredness.

Jeri had tried what the pastor suggested, but her depression didn't lift, and this raised some questions.

She noted that there was a history of depression among the women in her family and that she was presently experiencing some physical problems.

"My pastor says I'm in rebellion against God."

Moreover, she confided to her pastor that she was struggling in her relationship with her husband because he shrugged off responsibilities with their two teenagers, who were beginning to get into trouble.

The authors continued with Jeri's story:

> "How did the pastor respond when you said his suggestion didn't help?"
>
> "That's when he dropped the bomb on me," Jeri said.
>
> The counselor did not fail to notice her choice of metaphor—the devastation Jeri was trying to portray—and asked, "What sort of 'bomb'?"
>
> The pastor had told her, "The fact that you won't accept my counsel without raising all these objections and other possibilities was the major indication to me, Jeri, that your root problem is spiritual, not physical or emotional. When you talked about arguing with your husband, rather than submitting to him and trusting God, that confirmed it." He concluded that the other problems—emotional depression, physical illness, a troubled marriage and teenagers in turmoil—were the result of her inability to submit fully to God and His Word.
>
> Jeri had tried to object. "I told him I felt

19

condemned. That I felt I needed some other kind of help."

"What happened?" the counselor prompted.

"That made it worse. My pastor just smiled and said I wasn't willing to accept his counsel—so that proved he was right. That's when he used the 'R' word on me. He said, 'Jeri, you need to repent of your rebellion against God. Then all these minor problems will be taken care of.'"

"That's a strong judgment against you," the counselor noted. "What do you think about it?"

Tears welled up, and Jeri dabbed at them with a tissue. Then she sat wringing the tissue in knots as she replied. "I feel like a bug pinned down to a piece of cardboard. I try to praise God—I do praise Him. But the problem with my husband and kids goes on and on. And when I'm honest with myself I get mad, because just repeating Scriptures, when our family and our health are falling apart, seems so shallow.

"But then I wake up in the middle of the night, hearing my pastor's words. And I think I must be a terrible Christian—in rebellion, like he said—or my life wouldn't be such a mess. He's right, isn't he? Rebellion is a sin we all deal with.

"But the turmoil in me has gone on for four months, and I found myself thinking I should stick my head in our gas oven. And other times I think I must be on the verge of a breakthrough to more 'holiness'—if only I could praise enough or submit enough. But I don't think I can stick it out long enough. I just feel exhausted, and like I'm losing my mind.

20

"I can't carry all this weight any more," she ended, pleadingly. "Help me."

"Submit and obey"

One woman broke down in tears as she confessed to her ladies' Bible study group that her husband, who was not a Christian, had been trying to get her to attend sex parties where the men swap wives. Because of his persistent demand for her to obey and have sex with these men, she was looking for support in the face of this horrendous situation.

Instead of finding the support she needed, she was told by the leader of the Bible study that she needed to submit to her husband's authority—period.

The Bible study leader quoted 1 Peter 3:1, 6, which reads:

> Wives, likewise, be submissive to your own husbands, that even if some do not obey the word, they, without a word, may be won by the conduct of their wives...as Sarah obeyed Abraham, calling him lord, whose daughters you are, if you do good and are not afraid with any terror.

21

The Bible study leader was merely reflecting what was taught from the pulpit by the pastor—women were to submit to their husbands even if they were asked to commit sin. From verse 6 the church leaders rationalized that when Sarah called Abraham "lord," it referred to the time when, at Abraham's insistence, Sarah obediently consented to join Abimelech's harem. God delivered Sarah, and she was spared from having sex with Abimelech. When the incident was over, God rebuked Abraham for his sin.

As a result, the woman's Bible study group believed

that even if her husband asked his wife to have sex with the men at sex parties, like Sarah, she was to obey. Because she was simply obeying her "spiritual head,"

It is hard to imagine that the very organization— this sacred institution— established by God to help His sheep, His people, has become a system that wounds and hurts God's own.

the judgment for that sin would come upon the husband, and she would not be responsible. Thankfully, this lady refused their counsel. Eventually she had to leave the church to escape the constant judgment concerning her "rebellion" to her husband by her refusal to fornicate with his friends.

22

YES, SPIRITUAL ABUSE IS A PROBLEM!

Sadly, these are just a few examples of the lives that have been marred by a spirit of manipulation and control. Some of these individuals have never fully recovered from the abuse. Some still have not been able to admit to themselves that they are in an abusive church.

Understandably, spiritual abuse in the church is a difficult subject with which to grapple. It requires unveiling a problem within the sacred institution of the church. It is hard to imagine that the very organization—this sacred institution—established by God to help His sheep, His people, has become a system that wounds and hurts God's own. Because of this fact, as well as the fear of the backlash in exposing this spirit of control, we have kept silent. I believe it is time for the silence to be broken! Only by facing this issue honestly can we begin to stop the control and manipulation that has affected so many lives.

23

1. "Letters," *Charisma* (April 1999): 8.
2. Ibid., 10.
3. The story of Jeri is used with permission from *The Subtle Power of Spiritual Abuse* by David Johnson and Jeff VanVonderen, copyright © 1991 Bethany House Publishers, pages 16–19. All rights reserved.

QUESTIONS

Chapter 1
Is the Emperor Really Naked?

1. Have you or someone close to you ever experienced any form of spiritual abuse in a church or ministry setting? If so, describe what happened.

_____

_____

_____

_____

_____

2. Explain why you think some church leaders feel they must exert authoritarian control over their congregations.

_____

_____

_____

_____

_____

3. Why is it spiritually unhealthy for a pastor to tell his church members that they cannot visit other church services or participate in inter-church meetings?

_____

_____

_____

_____

_____

4. Discuss the situation involving the woman named Jeri (page 18), who was told she was in rebellion because she did not memorize a list of Scriptures to cure her depression. What was fundamentally wrong with this pastor's advice?

_____

_____

_____

_____

_____

_____

_____

5. If a church leader told a woman that she should submit to her husband's authority even if her husband is demanding that she do something immoral, how would you respond?

_____

_____

_____

_____

_____

_____

_____

_____

_____

_____

WARNING SIGNS OF AN ABUSIVE SYSTEM

WARNING:
SPIRITUAL ABUSE AHEAD

To enforce the pastor's authority, there had to be some form of punishment applied. This couple was then informed that no one from the church was permitted to speak to them or have any contact with them for a time determined by the pastor. Even their children were not permitted to play with any of the other children from the church.

The idea of spiritual abuse is not a new phenomenon. In the Old Testament, God spoke against those who operated in their own authority while abusing the very people they were to bless. In Jeremiah 5:30–31 we read, "An astonishing and horrible thing has been committed in the land: the prophets prophesy falsely, and the priests rule by their own power; and My people love to have it so. But what will you do in the end?"

In these verses God is bringing an indictment against the religious leaders of the Old Testament. We see the Lord's anger expressed against those who operate in their own authority. Consumed with their own ambition, these leaders have convinced the people that their power is divine. Yet in reality, these false prophets are merely wielding their self-imposed influence for personal gain, claiming they speak for God.

In Jeremiah 6:13–14 we read again of self-absorbed prophets and priests who are so preoccupied with their own needs being met that the needs of the people are being ignored. We read: "From the least of them even to the greatest of them, everyone is greedy for gain, and from the prophet even to the priest everyone deals falsely. And they have healed the brokenness of My people superficially, saying, 'Peace, peace,' but there is no peace" (NAS).

A common characteristic of an abusive religious system is that the real needs of the people are lost in the never-ending quest by the leaders for personal fulfillment and happiness.

The tragic story of Diane, a young woman in her late teens who had recently given her life to Christ, illustrates this point. Diane went on a missions trip with a group from the church she had been attending. One

29

day the missions team was enjoying some recreation time when Diane suffered a tragic accident that caused her leg to be so severely injured it was necessary to amputate it.

A common characteristic of an abusive religious system is that the real needs of the people are lost in the never-ending quest by the leaders for personal fulfillment and happiness.

Diane's parents were not Christians, and in the past they had somewhat resented the amount of time Diane had been spending at the church. When the accident occurred, their response was to blame the church for Diane's injury. They also felt the church should do something financially to help Diane.

During the time Diane was recovering in the hospital, her mother happened to hear the senior pastor of Diane's church describing the new, sporty car he intended to purchase. She began to tell people in the community about "this preacher who is living high on the church's money." Word got back to the pastor, and needless to say, he was not happy.

After several weeks in the hospital, Diane was transferred to a rehab facility. While she was in rehab the pastor came to see Diane. Diane was still wheelchair bound because she had not yet been fitted with a prosthesis.

After the initial greetings and some brief small talk, the pastor brought up to Diane what her mom was saying around town. The pastor advised Diane that her "assignment" was to talk to her mother and get her to stop gossiping about the pastor. Although Diane was still trying to process the idea of facing the rest of her life without a leg, by the time the pastor left, it was clear to her that her pastor had nothing to say to her to help her face the horrible physical and emotional issues brought on by her accident.

One of the church's staff members made a suggestion that the church buy Diane a prosthesis for her leg. Initially, the pastor vehemently opposed the idea. However, after some time, just to help smooth things over with Diane's mom, the pastor reluctantly consented to the purchase.

Diane's pastor failed to respond to Diane in a way that honored God. In fact, his response was more like that of the Pharisees of the New Testament, whom Jesus openly confronted concerning the way they treated others. As you read the New Testament, it doesn't take a tremendous amount of insight to see that the confrontations Jesus had were not with tax collectors, adulteresses, prostitutes or other "sinners." His confrontations were with the religious leaders and the religious system of His day.

In speaking of the Pharisees, Jesus said, "For they bind heavy burdens, hard to bear, and lay them on men's shoulders; but they themselves will not move them with one of their fingers" (Matt. 23:4). The Amplified Bible paints an even clearer picture. It says, "They tie up heavy loads, hard to bear, and place them on men's shoulders, but they themselves will not lift a finger to help bear them." Jesus is referring to the people's being weighted down by rules and regulations

31

that needed to be performed in order to gain the acceptance of the Pharisees. In the same way, many believers today have found themselves crushed beneath the religious baggage of an abusive system. Each day thousands of church members find themselves struggling to earn the favor and approval of a modern-day Pharisee.

Jesus cared deeply about His people—and how they were treated. When He saw the multitudes, "He was moved with compassion for them, because they were weary and scattered, like sheep having no shepherd" (Matt. 9:36). The Amplified Version expands on the word *weary* by saying, "They were bewildered (harassed and distressed and dejected and helpless), like sheep without a shepherd."

Notice that Jesus saw them as *harassed.* This word conveys the idea of some outside force pressing upon the people, causing them to feel weary, distressed and downcast. This outside force was the religious system that placed its emphasis on *outward appearances.* It was a system that promised peace based on one's ability to follow the prescribed rules and regulations. If one failed, then there was judgment.

Not having a shepherd didn't mean that the people lacked for those who told them what to do. There were plenty of Pharisees willing to do that. It meant they had no one to lead them to spiritual green pastures. A shepherd doesn't *drive* his sheep as cattlemen drive their cattle. A shepherd *leads* his sheep to a safe place where food is plentiful and where they can find rest.

Is it any wonder Jesus said:

> Come to Me, all you who labor and are heavy laden, and I will give you rest. Take My yoke

upon you and learn from Me, for I am gentle and lowly in heart, and you will find rest for your souls. For My yoke is easy and My burden is light.
—MATTHEW 11:28–30

A healthy church should produce peace and rest for your soul. Establishing healthy spiritual relationships will always be a challenge, but the process will prevent

Each day thousands of church members find themselves struggling to earn the favor and approval of a modern-day Pharisee.

you from becoming weary and worn, trying to jump through religious hoops that promise God's acceptance and love. If, in order to gain the acceptance of its leaders, your church constantly requires more and more of your life with no end in sight—and little encouragement along the way—then you may want to reexamine the church you are attending.

God's intention all along has been for the local church to be healthy, life giving and Christ centered. But because He has chosen to use frail, sin-prone individuals to lead His church, there is always the possibility that a local congregation can fall into deception or unhealthy spiritual patterns.

WARNING SIGNS

So how do you know whether a church has come

33

under the influence of a controlling spirit? There are some clear warning signs that can signal an atmosphere of abuse.

POWER POSITIONING

There is certainly a place for biblical teaching on spiritual authority. But if a pastor preaches on this subject every Sunday, constantly reminding everyone that he is in charge, you can be sure that trouble is around the corner.

In an unhealthy church, the pastor actually begins to take the place of Jesus in people's lives. Commonly, people are told they cannot leave the church with God's blessing unless the pastor approves the decision. The implication is that unless they receive pastoral permission, not only will God not bless them, but they will also be cursed in some way, resulting in sure failure. Controlling spiritual leaders use this kind of reasoning to manipulate people.

We must understand the process a church goes through to reach this point of deception. Because many pastors measure their success through church attendance, they may become disappointed if people leave their church. If they are insecure, they may actually develop a doctrine in order to stop people from leaving. They may preach sermons about unconditional loyalty, using the biblical stories of David and Jonathan, or Elisha and Elijah.

By using examples like these, the leader can actually gain "biblical" grounds to control even the personal areas of his parishioners. A controlling leader may also attempt to instill a sense of obligation by reminding his congregation of everything he has done for them.

This kind of preaching causes church members to

seek a position of favor with the pastor rather than a proper desire to "please God and not man." Jesus also condemned such man-pleasing when He told the Pharisees, "I have come in My Father's name, and you do not receive Me...How can you believe, who receive honor from one another, and do not seek the honor

In an unhealthy church, the pastor actually begins to take the place of Jesus in people's lives.

that comes from the only God?" (John 5:43–44).

When we pursue the honor of men, we do so at the expense of our relationship with God. If we continue to do so, gradually men will take the place of God in our lives. An unhealthy soul tie is created, and our sense of confidence is determined by our standing with those in leadership. This kind of control will destroy people spiritually!

35

A healthy church will not allow genuine pastoral concern to cross the line into manipulation or control. A true shepherd will use his influence to draw church members into a closer relationship with Jesus, who is the only "head of the church" (Eph. 5:23). A true shepherd realizes that the people in his congregation don't belong to him—they are God's flock.

UNQUESTIONED AUTHORITY

In an unhealthy church, it is considered rebellion when someone questions decisions that are made or statements that are said from the pulpit. Granted, there are those who constantly question the leadership in any church—but often such constant questioning comes from an individual's critical attitude. Pastors must learn to deal with such questioning in a compassionate, positive manner. However, in an unhealthy church, any and all questions are considered threats to the pastor's "God-ordained" authority. Members who do dare to question their leaders or who do not follow their directives often are confronted with severe consequences.

A man from one church told me, "We were told that it is more important to obey leaders than to question what they are doing." He went on to say, "It was unthinkable to question the motives of the pastor."

For example, one couple, members of a church on the West Coast, decided to take a family vacation. This couple purchased their airline tickets and finalized the rest of their plans. They were looking forward to their long-needed time off. Once the pastor discovered their plans, he rebuked them for not getting his permission first and warned them not to go on the trip. They went anyway. Shortly after they returned, they were visited by some of the church's leadership. They were informed that by going on vacation against the pastor's wishes, they were in rebellion. To enforce the pastor's authority, there had to be some form of punishment applied. This couple was then informed that no one from the church was permitted to speak to them or have any contact with them for a time determined by the pastor. Even their children were not permitted to play with any of the other children from the church.

Pastors operating under a spirit of control are often convinced that they are the only ones who can accurately hear from God. Under the constant exposure to

36

this spirit, members often become convinced that they indeed need their pastor to think for them. In essence, their personal fellowship with the Lord has been abdicated for a relationship with a man. As a result they lose their confidence in being able to discern the will of God for their lives.

It is very simple—money represents power. It should be no surprise that controlling leaders will use unbiblical means to manipulate people into giving.

An atmosphere of secrecy

Once a church member surrenders to a system of control, the leader gives limited information to each individual, carefully monitoring each relationship. As a result, each member is only able to relate to other members based on the information he receives from the leader.

37

In this way, if the church staff or pastor determines that one of the members has become a "threat," they have a strategy in place to maintain the control they believe is required. Consequently the church can sever relationships when necessary and keep this process cloaked behind a veil of secrecy.

This is not limited to members of the congregation. I know a pastor who did this with his staff. In casual conversations he would make a comment that would result in one staff member becoming suspicious of another. Or he would say something to cause one staff member to feel superior.

This atmosphere fueled selfish ambition and competition among the staff. It became the pastor's way of maintaining control and ensuring that his staff could never challenge his authority. In time, the assistant pastors discovered what was happening, and eventually they all left.

Secrecy may also cloak the area of finances. Pastors may make brazen appeals for money, yet offer no assurance that the finances of the church are handled with accountability and integrity.

I have actually heard pastors tell their congregations that the financial decisions of the church do not become a public matter because "the congregation doesn't have the spiritual insight or maturity to understand the dynamics of church finances." Have you heard this line of reasoning before?

Some pastors actually preach, "It doesn't matter what we do with your money. Your responsibility is simply to give." However, the Bible commands us to be good stewards—and part of good stewardship is making sure that proper systems of accountability are established to handle tithes and offerings. (See 1 Peter 4:10.)

It is very simple—money represents power. Ultimately, control comes down to issues of power. Therefore, it should be no surprise that controlling leaders will use unbiblical means to manipulate people into giving.

As good stewards, when we become aware of financial mismanagement, we are responsible for where we sow our financial seed. I can't imagine anyone choosing to continue to give money after becoming aware of the misuse of funds. However, if the approval of those in leadership is more important to a person than financial integrity, that person might still feel compelled to give—even if misuse of funds was involved.

AN ELITIST ATTITUDE

The deadly trait of elitism produces an "us and them" mentality. A church with an elitist attitude believes "no one else" is really preaching the gospel—except that church. Or at least, no one is preaching it *as effectively* as they are!

An elitist spirit discourages church members from visiting other churches or receiving counsel from anyone who doesn't attend their church. If anyone visits another church, he is viewed as a dissident.

"Everything you need can be found within the framework of our group," this spirit says, adding, "Everything you need to know, you will receive from the pastor and his teachings." Consequently there is little respect, if any, for other denominations or church groups.

One individual, in speaking about the elitist attitude within his church, said, "Although we didn't come right out and say it, in our innermost hearts we really felt there was no place like our assembly. We thought the rest of Christianity was out to lunch."

39

Another man from the same church said, "When a well-known evangelical speaker was preaching in another church in the area, the leaders would discourage us from attending. Also, if the leaders found out that members were considering visiting another church for any reason, they were called in and chastised. 'You don't need to be going to those other churches,' they would tell us. 'The ministry here is rich enough. Isn't the Lord feeding you here?'"

A healthy church respects and celebrates the other expressions of Christ's many-membered body. A Jesus-centered church realizes that no one denomination or local church can win a city, regardless of how large it is. Christ-centered leaders who are clothed with humility recognize that the small church is as significant as the large church, the Baptists are as vital as the Charismatics, and every racial group has a place at the Lord's table.

A healthy church will promote other churches in the city, rather than simply promoting its own events and agendas all the time. A healthy church will promote spiritual renewal in all churches rather than further the idea that it has some kind of doctrinal superiority. A healthy church will exude the attitude described in Philippians 2:3–4:

> Let nothing be done through selfish ambition or conceit, but in lowliness of mind let each esteem others better than himself. Let each of you look out not only for his own interests, but also the interests of others.

40

PERFORMANCE EMPHASIS

Opportunities to minister are abundant in most churches. Yet in a controlling church, individual areas of ministry are no longer opportunities to serve. They become necessary in order to prove one's commitment to the organization. Whether it is faithful attendance to worship services or working in some department, proving one's loyalty becomes the key.

Obviously church attendance is vital to our spiritual growth. But if we find ourselves attending church so we can win favor with the pastor or to earn his trust, then we have missed the point.

Galatians 2:16 tells us, "A man is not justified by the

works of the law but by faith in Jesus Christ." We cannot earn heaven or God's love. The message of God's grace doesn't cancel the need to serve—it just exposes the "why" of our service.

Even though we are instructed to engage in certain disciplines in the Christian life, these disciplines are not a means of gaining God's acceptance. They are meant to be a celebration of His unconditional love and mercy.

FEAR MOTIVATION

When a pastor tells his congregation that those who leave his church or disobey his authority are in danger of God's wrath, you can be sure this man is operating in a spirit of control. He is attempting to use fear as a carnal means of keeping people in his church. The line usually goes like this: "If you leave our church, the blessing of God will be lifted from your life, and you will miss God's will." Another version says, "If you leave our church, you will be in rebellion, and Satan will be free to bring havoc into your life."

Fear is the motivation behind such comments—*not love.* You can be sure that this type of reasoning is not from God. Jesus never motivated men out of fear. In a controlling church, fear is a form of manipulation. Instead of motivating people through love and servanthood, a controlling church tries to motivate through manipulation.

Motivating people through fear is a direct contradiction to 1 John 4:18, which says, "There is no fear in love; but perfect love casts out fear."

PAINFUL EXIT

In a controlling church, it is impossible to leave on good terms. Because the pastor's sense of worth is

41

usually based on the control he is able to exert over the congregation, when someone leaves, this insecure leader considers it an affront to his leadership. Therefore he often takes it personally. As a result, when people do leave, they are labeled rebellious, or the rest of the congregation is given the explanation that they left because they had become offended.

In an unhealthy church, there is never a good reason why anyone should leave. Regardless of the situation, the people who leave are always the "problem."

This truism present in abusive churches applies not only to members, but to church staff as well. In one particular church, each time a staff member left, the senior pastor did his best to cast a shadow over that person's reputation in the hope that it would destroy any chance of that person succeeding without him someplace else.

Tyrone was a youth minister at a church like this. One of the first conflicts he had with the senior pastor took place after a special youth outreach that Tyrone headed up. It was a skateboard outreach. Tyrone went over the idea and details with the senior pastor, informing the pastor that the outreach would require bringing in a guest speaker.

Once everything was given the OK, Tyrone proceeded with the outreach. It was a bigger success than anyone had anticipated. Approximately two thousand kids came for the different skateboard rallies that were held over a period of three days.

But instead of being excited about the results, the senior pastor became angry. He told Tyrone that he was unhappy with the event because "it took over the whole church." Tyrone suspected that the pastor felt upstaged by the response. "It was the talk of the church for some time," Tyrone said.

Tyrone went on to clarify, "I came on staff there not only to build a successful youth ministry, but also to be

Instead of motivating people through love and servanthood, a controlling church tries to motivate through manipulation.

mentored in the things of ministry." Tyrone continued by saying that this position was his first ministry position, and he knew he had a lot to learn. But he was willing to do so.

It soon became apparent that the pastor had a different idea concerning Tyrone's position. Tyrone discovered that his job description also involved shoveling the pastor's drive, picking up his dry cleaning, starting his car for him in the winter and cleaning out his pool in the summer. "I didn't mind doing any of that," Tyrone said. "I was just expecting more input from the pastor in the area of ministry."

43

Tyrone continued by explaining, "A lot of the conflict was due to our differing perspectives concerning my position as well as our views about ministry." After about one year, it was mutually decided that it would be better if Tyrone resigned in light of "philosophical differences" between the senior pastor and himself.

Tyrone told the pastor that after resigning, he would be moving to Kentucky. He asked the pastor if he could use him as a reference when he applied for another position. The senior pastor assured Tyrone that he would give him a positive recommendation. However, before Tyrone and his wife moved to Kentucky, a staff member of the church delivered a statement typed out on the church's letterhead. The statement was an explanation as to why Tyrone was "discharged" from his position as youth pastor.

The Good Shepherd is fully able to lead you into a green pasture where you can grow in your relationship with Him.

Tyrone and his wife were shocked. Based on their previous conversation, Tyrone was under the impression that they had reached a mutual decision that being there at the church just wasn't a good "fit." The statement described all the things that Tyrone had done wrong while he was at that church and stated that the senior pastor didn't believe Tyrone was "ministry material." It also said that Tyrone did not have a servant's heart and that the pastor even seriously doubted the validity of Tyrone's relationship with God.

Shortly after Tyrone and his wife arrived in Kentucky, Tyrone heard of a job opening in a church in their new city. He applied in person for the position and left the pastor his résumé. Within a few days, they met with the pastor of this new church. He informed Tyrone that when the church board called the previous church about a recommendation, his former church sent the same letter they gave Tyrone before he left. Based on such a poor recommendation, the pastor informed Tyrone that they could not consider him for the position.

Shortly after this incident, Tyrone and his wife started a church in Kentucky. Ten years later their church is thriving and healthy.

Many times in an abusive church you will hear the pastor declare curses over the lives of those who have left. Accusations are made against their character, and other members are strongly discouraged from having any contact with the former members. I heard one pastor, while preaching, refer to a former staff member as a spiritual "whore" because he left and took another ministry position in another state. It is true that many people leave churches for the wrong reasons. But in a controlling church, rarely—if ever—is anyone truly blessed by the leadership as they leave.

WHAT CAN I DO ABOUT IT?

How should you respond if your church displays one or more of these unhealthy traits? Here's some advice:

- Talk with your pastor or someone else in leadership about your concerns, keeping in mind that if he is truly motivated by a spirit of control you may encounter some manipulation during the conversation. Stay in a humble attitude rather than getting angry or defensive.

45

- A controlling church leader will discourage you from speaking with anyone else about your concerns. However, the Bible says that "in the multitude of counselors there is safety" (Prov. 11:14). Seek counsel from a mature, objective leader in another church or another mature Christian. It is possible that what you have perceived as a controlling attitude may be genuine concern—so pray for discernment.

- If after receiving counsel you are convinced that your church is in the grip of a controlling spirit, then you are free to leave. You are not responsible for anyone else who is still loyal to the church, so don't try to rescue them. Pray for those people to discern the situation.

- At first you may feel that you can't trust another pastor again, but resist those thoughts and find a healthy church where the life of God is flowing, where the Bible is preached without compromise and where love is evident.

One couple went through the process of leaving an abusive church. The pastor did everything he could to discredit them and malign their character. Initially, they both were frightened that they would be blacklisted from every church in their community. At first, they wanted to defend their character. It seemed that this pastor continued to have control over their lives even after they left. They wondered if they would ever be able to escape his influence.

Finally, they realized that God was their defense and protection. Instead of defending themselves, they decided to pray for their former pastor. The more they prayed for him, the less threatening he became in their minds. The anger they first had toward the pastor was replaced with compassion. As time passed, they realized that he didn't have as much influence as they initially thought. Because they had kept their hearts pure, they were able to find another church and to continue to grow spiritually.

There is life after spiritual abuse. You may be

tempted to feel that you will never escape the controlling grasp of an abusive leader. Satan will cause you to think that the controlling leader's influence is greater than it really is. Don't give in to Satan's intimidation. Trust God to be your strength and your defense. Keep your heart tender. Pray for those who have used you, and bless those who have cursed you. If you will do these things, you will discover a sure path that God has prepared for you as well as His destiny for your life.

God has a healthy church for you. The Good Shepherd is fully able to lead you into a green pasture where you can grow in your relationship with Him (Ps. 23:2). As you allow Him to lead you, He will also anoint your head with oil, healing any wounds you encountered in an abusive environment (v. 5).

QUESTIONS

Chapter 2
Warning Signs of an Abusive System

1. Read Jeremiah 6:13–14. Why is it that abusive church leaders cannot heal the people they are leading?

   _____

   _____

   _____

2. Read the description of Jesus in Matthew 9:36 and 11:28–30. How should these verses provide a model for a Christian leader's behavior?

   _____

   _____

   _____

3. Many Christians easily fall into the trap of drawing all their strength from a pastor or spiritual mentor, and as a result, their relationship with God suffers. How can we avoid this?

   _____

   _____

   _____

4. When is it necessary to seek pastoral counsel about an important life decision?

   _____

   _____

   _____

5. Why is it unbiblical for a pastor to suggest that he must "hear God" for a person in his church?

_____

_____

_____

_____

_____

6. How would you respond if a pastor told you that members of his congregation are not allowed to know anything about the financial decisions of the church? Should the congregation know how much money the pastor makes?

_____

_____

_____

_____

_____

7. Some abusive leaders tell members of their churches that if they leave the congregation the blessing of God will be lifted from their lives. Why is this unbiblical?

_____

_____

_____

_____

_____

TRAITS OF AN ABUSIVE LEADER

WARNING:
SPIRITUAL ABUSE AHEAD

I found it troubling that the pastor had attempted to produce the *perfect* church by creating a close-knit community governed by strict rules, stern authority and intense loyalty. The newspaper quoted one former member as saying, "You just didn't question anything that was said or done. The church demanded blind loyalty."

A newspaper in one Midwestern city has run several stories about an independent church located within the city. One story told about a lawsuit filed against the church concerning fraud. The lawsuit accused the church of attracting children to their services with the promise of trinkets and fun activities, only to baptize many of them without their parents' permission. A jury cleared the church of the most serious charges involved in the suit, but found the church did deceive eight children. It was ordered to pay damages to each child.

Another story, which ran in another newspaper about this same church, reported the arrest, conviction and consequential prison sentence of one of the pastor's sons for sexual abuse. It had been discovered that over the years, the son had engaged in sexual relations with several teenage girls—all members of his father's congregation.

In addition to these discoveries, I found it troubling that the pastor had attempted to produce the *perfect* church by creating a close-knit community governed by strict rules, stern authority and intense loyalty. The newspaper quoted one former member as saying, "You just didn't question anything that was said or done. The church demanded blind loyalty."

When the local newspaper interviewed one of the pastor's daughters, she explained her father's strong control and strict rules by saying, "I think the reason he had his standards was to be different from most churches. He felt that was what God wanted us to live like. The standards gave him a basis of control. It gave him power and respect." The daughter went on to say, "In my heart, I have always felt that the church was my father's greatest love."

53

The highly regimented environment in this independent church includes not only abstinence from any alcohol and tobacco, but abstinence from involvement in bowling leagues, mixed swimming and the movies. Members are also commanded to avoid association with anyone who is involved in such activities.

One former member remembers a sermon that the pastor preached about the importance of male and female separation. This former member described the pastor holding up a lollipop, commenting on how good it looked and how it was nicely wrapped. The pastor unwrapped the lollipop and began to lick it. Then the pastor addressed the girls in the audience, making this statement: "That's what you are doing when you let a boy kiss you. You're tainted—like gum someone else has chewed."

In another sermon, this pastor boldly declared his expectation to exercise control in even the most personal aspects of his congregants' lives. He stated that the people needed to check with him before they made any large purchases. He went on to describe a large purchase as being one of one hundred dollars or more.

A spirit of control, fueled by a heart of insecurity, drives men like this pastor. Unfortunately, this spirit has been around a long time, and it has a long list of men who have succumbed to its seduction of absolute power.

SAUL—PORTRAIT OF AN INSECURE LEADER

One of the saddest examples of an abusive leader is found in the life of King Saul. Saul's life is a tragic testimony of a man who had everything, and yet lost it all because of his insecurity. First Samuel 31:4 paints a picture of the tragic end to Saul's life:

Then Saul said to his armorbearer, "Draw your sword, and thrust me through with it, lest these uncircumcised men come and thrust me through and abuse me." But his armor-bearer would not, for he was greatly afraid. Therefore Saul took a sword and fell on it.

As tragic as was the end of Saul's reign, the beginning was just the opposite. The people of Israel approached the prophet Samuel asking for a king to be set over them. Each time they asked, Samuel took

A spirit of control, fueled by a heart of insecurity, drives men like this pastor.

Israel's request to the Lord. Each time God instructed Samuel to explain to Israel that He was their King.

But this wasn't good enough for the people of Israel—they demanded that Samuel set a king over them. Why were the people of Israel so persistent in their request for a king? Because they wanted be like the other nations. Finally, God relented. We read God's response in 1 Samuel 8:21–22:

> And Samuel heard all the words of the people, and he repeated them in the hearing of the LORD. So the LORD said to Samuel, "Heed their voice, and make them a king." And Samuel said to the man of Israel, "Every man go to his city."

It is important to see the chain of events that led up to Saul's becoming the king of Israel. What we will see

55

is that even though it wasn't God's desire for Israel to have a king over them, it is clear that God had provided everything Saul needed to succeed.

I have often heard it explained that Saul failed as a leader because, although David was *God's choice*, Saul was simply the *choice of the people*. But the Scriptures do not indicate that this is true. In 1 Samuel 9:15–16 we read:

> Now the LORD had told Samuel in his ear the day before Saul came, saying, "Tomorrow about this time I will send you a man from the land of Benjamin, and you shall anoint him commander over My people Israel, that he may save My people from the hand of the Philistines; for I have looked upon My people, because their cry has come to Me."

And then, just in case the prophet did not recognize Saul as the man God had sent, the Lord said to Samuel, "There he is, the man of whom I spoke to you. This one shall reign over My people" (1 Sam. 9:17).

It is clear that out of all the men of Israel, God had chosen Saul to be Israel's first king. When God could have chosen anyone, He chose this lowly Benjamite. In God's selection, Saul discovered a validation he had never known, as well as a new sense of destiny and purpose he never had.

But God wasn't finished—if that wasn't enough to convince Saul and all of Israel of God's choice for a king, Samuel prophesied to Saul concerning an event that would take place, one that would dramatically change Saul's life. This event would so transform Saul that he would literally be "turned into another man."

> After that you shall come to the hill of God where

the Philistine garrison is. And it will happen,
when you have come there to the city, that you
will meet a group of prophets coming down from
the high place with a stringed instrument, a tam-
bourine, a flute, and a harp before them; and they
will be prophesying. Then the Spirit of the LORD
will come upon you, and you will prophesy with
them and be turned into another man.

—1 SAMUEL 10:5–6

In God's selection, Saul discovered a validation he had never known, as well as a new sense of destiny and purpose he never had.

After this prophecy from Samuel, we see how this
radical change would take place in Saul. In 1 Samuel
10:9 we read, "So it was, when he [Saul] had turned his
back to go from Samuel, that God gave him another
heart; and all those signs came to pass that day." The
reference note in my Bible says that God "changed his
heart." This again was a tangible demonstration of
God's love and acceptance of Saul. When God gives a
man or woman a new heart, it is a heart that is tender
to the things of God. When God gives someone a new
heart, it isn't going to be a hard heart, a selfish heart
or a cowardly heart. Certainly God isn't going to give
someone an insecure heart!

Yet, this wasn't the end of the blessings of God in
Saul's life. The inauguration service of Saul as king was

57

a time of further validation, and it also gives us some insights as to where Saul's life took a turn for the worse.

All of Israel gathered together for the event when Saul would be set in place as the nation's first king:

Fifty people can love and accept us, and yet our tendency when rejected is to forget the fifty and to focus on the one who has rejected us.

58

> And when Samuel had caused all the tribes of Israel to come near, the tribe of Benjamin was chosen. When he had caused the tribe of Benjamin to come near by their families, the family of Matri was chosen. And Saul the son of Kish was chosen. But when they sought him, he could not be found.
>
> —1 Samuel 10:20–21

Saul was so overwhelmed with his new position that he wasn't sure how to respond. Consequently, Saul hid himself from the celebration. When they were unsuccessful in finding Saul, the Bible says they "inquired of the Lord" as to Saul's whereabouts. The Lord told them that Saul was "hiding among the equipment" (1 Sam. 10:22). In 1 Samuel 10:23–24 we read what happens next:

> So they ran and brought him [Saul] from there;

and when he stood among the people, he was taller than any of the people from his shoulders upward. And Samuel said to all the people, "Do you see him whom the LORD has chosen, that there is no one like him among the people?" So all the people shouted and said, "Long live the king!"

All of Israel declared their approval of Saul. Israel's collective voices must have sounded like thunder in Saul's ears. Israel also honored Saul by bringing him gifts.

In just a very short time, Saul had gone from a place of obscurity to a position of highest honor among his people. The dramatic events that changed Saul's life climaxed at the moment he was crowned king.

But during what should have been Saul's finest hour, an event unfolded that Satan used to poison Saul, eventually costing him the kingdom. In 1 Samuel 10:27 we read about this defining moment in Saul's life:

> But some rebels said, "How can this man save us?" So they despised him [Saul], and brought him no presents. But he held his peace.

59

The phrase "But he held his peace" is interesting. It implies that Saul noticed the rejection of these men. Out of all of Israel, these few rebellious men demonstrated their silent protest of Saul by refusing to bring him any gifts. And even though Saul held his peace, he allowed the rejection of these few men to poison his new heart. Isn't that a perfect example of the deception of human nature? Fifty people can love and accept us, and yet our tendency when rejected is to forget the fifty and to focus on the one who has rejected us.

Saul had an entire nation celebrating him. More importantly, the God of the universe had affirmed Saul with a magnificent expression of love. Yet Saul found his heart poisoned with fear because of the rejection of a few men. Consequently, Saul became imprisoned by the fear of rejection. It is very important to note that from this time forward, Saul's chief aim as king was to maintain the approval of the people of Israel.

Insecure leaders have a desperate need to be needed and a passion for the affirmation of man.

Traits of an Insecure Leader

There were three initial sins that Saul committed. After these three sins, the kingdom was taken from him. I call these transgressions committed by Saul *sins of insecurity*. Within these sins, and the events surrounding them, we will see four major traits of an insecure leader.

1. The lust of approbation

Initially, Saul started out strong in his reign as king. For example, in 1 Samuel 11 we see Saul saving Jabesh Gilead. By the time we get to 1 Samuel 13, Saul has reigned two years. It is after his second year as king that we see Saul committing his first sin of insecurity.

Saul had attacked a garrison of the Philistines. When the Philistines heard what Saul had done, they responded with force: "Then the Philistines gathered together to fight with Israel, thirty thousand chariots and six thousand horsemen, and people as the sand which is on the seashore in multitude" (1 Sam. 13:5).

60

As a result, when the men of Israel heard of the Philistines' plan to attack, they hid in caves, thickets, rocks—anywhere they could to save their lives. Some of the Hebrews crossed over Jordan to the land of Gad and Gilead. Saul was in Gilgal, and the Bible says that the people followed Saul as they trembled in fear (v. 7).

Because the Philistines had gathered for war, Saul knew that Israel would need to go into battle. The prophet Samuel was to come within seven days to offer a burnt offering. When Samuel didn't come within the seven days, Saul took matters into his own hands.

> Then he waited seven days, according to the time set by Samuel. But Samuel did not come to Gilgal; and the people were scattered from him. So Saul said, "Bring a burnt offering and peace offerings here to me." And he offered the burnt offering.
>
> —1 SAMUEL 13:8–9

Once Saul had performed the offering, Samuel arrived and Saul went out to meet him. Samuel immediately confronted Saul concerning his carrying out the burnt offering on his own. Within Saul's response, we see why he took matters in his own hands:

61

> And Samuel said, "What have you done?" Saul said, "When I saw that the people were scattered from me, and that you did not come within the days appointed, and that the Philistines gathered together at Michmash, then I said, 'The Philistines will now come down on me at Gilgal, and I have not made supplication to the LORD.' Therefore I felt compelled, and offered a burnt offering."
>
> —1 SAMUEL 13:11–12

Notice Saul said he was concerned that the people were "scattered" from him. For us to really understand what is going on in Saul's heart, we need to understand the significance of the burnt offering he initiated. According to the Law, the offering could only be performed by a prophet or priest. Samuel was the prophet of God to Israel. The carrying out of this offering by Saul was unlawful. In addition, once this offering was successfully completed, it represented the blessing of God, which was imperative to secure before Israel was to go into battle. Therefore, it is most important to recognize that in Saul's mind, the completion of the burnt offering would be an indication of God's approval and hand upon Saul, not only in the impending battle with the Philistines, but also as king.

When Samuel did not come to Gilgal in seven days as he had promised, the people of Israel, realizing the importance of an offering to God before battle, began to question the anointing on Saul's life: "Why hasn't Samuel arrived? Does this mean that God isn't going to be with Saul in the battle ahead of us?" As a result, they began to "scatter," as Saul put it.

Saul could see that he was quickly losing influence with the people. Because Saul had never gotten over the rejection of the men of Belial, he couldn't stand the thought of being rejected again. As a result, he took the path of expediency and offered up the burnt offering himself.

Out of his fear of rejection, Saul found himself living for the approval of others. He defined his personal worth based on what the people thought of him and how they responded to him. This deep-seated insecurity leads to the lust of approbation. When we are being driven by this compulsion, we find ourselves desperately needing others to affirm us. Insecure leaders need some kind of affirmation in order to feel good about themselves. If a leader's sense of worth isn't found in God's love, he constantly finds himself fishing for that pat on the back or that compliment. An insecure leader demands signs of inordinate loyalty—no matter what the cost may be to his followers. The lust of approbation demands constant recognition and validation from others to feel a sense of worth. Insecure leaders have a desperate need to be needed and a passion for the affirmation of man. Why? It is in the affirmation of others that they determine their personal value. Living for the approval of others is a sure sign of insecurity, and many times it leads to spiritual abuse.

2. COWARDICE

Even though, in response to Saul's attack upon the garrison of Philistines, the Philistines had encamped in a place called Michmash, Saul, Jonathan and six hundred men remained in Gibeah (1 Sam. 13:16). Soon, "raiders came out of the camp of the Philistines in three companies," traveling in three different directions (v. 17). The Philistine's strategy was to surround Saul and his men, positioning themselves for a sure victory. The Philistines were cocky and sure of success because of one other factor in their favor: "Now there was no blacksmith to be found throughout all the land of Israel, for the Philistines said, 'Lest the Hebrews make swords or spears'" (v. 19). Somehow the Philistines had successfully removed anyone from Israel who was able to make any weapons of war.

63

> So it came about, on the day of battle, that there was neither sword nor spear found in the hand of any of the people who were with Saul and

Jonathan. But they were found with Saul and
Jonathan his son.

—1 Samuel 13:22

Only Saul and Jonathan had any weapons for battle!
As a result, Saul, as well as the rest of the six hundred
men, was overcome with fear. Instead of courageously
leading his men into battle, Saul falls in a frightened

It should have been Saul who led Israel to victory. But when a man lives for the approval of others, he is enslaved to the fear of man.

heap under a pomegranate tree on the outskirts of
Gibeah (14:2).

In the meantime, Jonathan made a decision to enter
battle with God's help:

64

> Now it happened one day that Jonathan the son
> of Saul said to the young man who bore his
> armor, "Come, let us go over to the Philistines'
> garrison that is on the other side." But he did not
> tell his father.
>
> —1 Samuel 14:1

Jonathan and his armorbearer made their way to the
camp of the Philistines. Once the Philistines saw them,
they called out to Jonathan and the young man who
was with him: "Come up to us, and we will show you
something" (v. 12). But God had something bigger to

show—shortly afterward, twenty Philistines lay dead at the hand of Jonathan and his armorbearer. As a result, the Philistines were overcome with fear and began to scatter in terror. The watchmen for the people of Israel saw how the Philistines began to run in horror.

It was later discovered that it was Jonathan and his armorbearer who had struck such fear in the hearts of the Philistines.

While King Saul cowered in fear, his son Jonathan took the lead and brought victory to Israel through his simple act of courage. It should have been Saul who led Israel to victory. But when a man lives for the approval of others, he is enslaved to the fear of man. This translates not only in the fear of the rejection of friends, but also fear in the face of enemies. Often abusive leaders are afraid of direct and honest confrontation, preferring others to do their "dirty work." Because of their insecurities and personal inner conflicts, often they are incapable of straightforward communication. In his book *Principle-Centered Leadership*, Stephen Covey further explains this point:

65

> When you are living in harmony with your core values and principles, you can be straightforward, honest and up-front. And nothing is more disturbing to people who are full of trickery and duplicity than straightforward honesty—that's the one thing they can't deal with.[1]

3. JEALOUSY

Not wanting to be upstaged by his son Jonathan, and in an attempt to prove his own courage, Saul declared that no one was to eat until he killed his quota of Philistines. Although Israel was weak from hunger, no one ate because of Saul's oath. However, the problem was that Jonathan didn't hear his father's decree, for he was busy establishing victory for Israel by destroying the Philistines. After doing so, Jonathan came to the forest where the people of Israel had gathered. The forest was filled with honey, both on the ground and dripping from the abundance of honeycombs.

As Jonathan entered the forest he dipped his staff in a honeycomb and began to eat the honey. The people of Israel gasped in disbelief, saying, "Your father strictly charged the people with an oath, saying, 'Cursed is the man who eats food this day'" (1 Sam. 14:28).

Jonathan responded in this way:

> My father has troubled the land. Look now, how my countenance has brightened because I tasted a little of this honey. How much better if the people had eaten freely today of the spoil of their enemies which they found! For now would there not have been a much greater slaughter among the Philistines?
>
> —1 Samuel 14:29–30

66

Because of Jonathan's courage and the fear that struck the hearts of the Philistines, Israel drove back the Philistines from Michmash all the way to Aijalon. Consequently, there was a great spoil of sheep, oxen and calves. The people had not eaten due to Saul's decree, and they were faint with hunger. They began to eat sheep, oxen and calves—with the blood, which was unlawful to do.

The priests immediately informed Saul of the people's sin of eating the flesh of the herds with the blood. Quickly, Saul built an altar in order to make a sacrifice for the sin of the people. Then Saul attempted to determine who was to blame for the people's sin.

Through a biblical system of the casting of lots, the lot fell to Jonathan, indicating his guilt. "Tell me what you have done," Saul demanded of Jonathan. Jonathan replied by telling his father that he had simply eaten a little honey from the end of his staff. Realizing the implication of the casting of lots, he added, "So now I must die!"

We constantly find the need to decrease the value of others through criticism, thinking that by reducing their worth, we increase our own.

Saul answered, "God do so and more also; for you shall surely die, Jonathan" (v. 44). Jonathan was stunned and confused by his father's anger and found it hard to believe that his own father would kill him over this.

At this point the people of Israel finally took a stand against their own king.

67

> But the people said to Saul, "Shall Jonathan die, who has accomplished this great deliverance in Israel? Certainly not! As the LORD lives, not one hair of his head shall fall to the ground, for he has worked with God this day." So the people rescued Jonathan, and he did not die.
>
> —1 SAMUEL 14:45

It wasn't Jonathan who caused the people to sin by devouring animals—blood and all. It was Saul's ungodly decree of withholding food from Israel in a time of battle. It was Saul's impulsive edict that brought Israel to the point of near starvation. That is why the people began to eat the sheep, oxen and calves along with the blood.

However, there is always a penalty for sin, and as a result of Israel's sin, Saul needed to find someone to blame. Because of his intense insecurity, Saul felt he couldn't afford to take responsibility for his own actions and honestly face his own cowardice. Therefore, he needed someone upon whom to point the finger of blame. It was a spirit of jealousy that drove Saul to lay charge against his own son, even to the point of being willing to kill Jonathan.

If we are insecure, any praise or recognition that others receive, we view as a threat to our own sense of worth. Somehow we feel that the recognition of others diminishes our value. Therefore, we constantly find the need to decrease the value of others through criticism, thinking that by reducing their worth, we increase our own. Saul lived under this deception—as does any insecure leader.

68

4. OVERLY CONCERNED WITH APPEARANCES

Another characteristic of insecure leadership is a preoccupation with image. If, because of insecurity, a leader determines his or her worth or value based on the opinions of others, it is vitally important to that person that others think well of him or her. Someone with a spirit of insecurity can't afford to show any weakness for fear that it will result in some form of rejection. Therefore, many times it is necessary to craft an image that doesn't always reflect the truth.

The truth doesn't matter as much to an insecure leader as appearance. Why? Because that person believes in the power of appearance to establish the opinions of others.

Again, we see this trait in the life of King Saul. In 1 Samuel 15:1–3, Samuel brings Saul a message from the Lord concerning Amalek.

> Samuel also said to Saul, "The LORD sent me to anoint you king over His people, over Israel. Now, therefore, heed the voice of the words of the LORD. Thus says the LORD of hosts: 'I will punish Amalek for what he did to Israel, how he ambushed him on the way when he came up from Egypt. Now go and attack Amalek, and utterly destroy all that they have, and do not spare them. But kill both man and woman, infant and nursing child, ox and sheep, camel and donkey.'"

The instructions that Saul received were clear and simple. He was to completely destroy the Amalekites, sparing nothing or anyone. Yet as simple as the command of the Lord was, Saul once again chose to do his own thing, deviating from the command of God.

69

> And Saul attacked the Amalekites, from Havilah all the way to Shur, which is east of Egypt. He also took Agag king of the Amalekites alive, and utterly destroyed all the people with the edge of the sword. But Saul and the people spared Agag and the best of the sheep, the oxen, the fatlings, the lambs, and all that was good, and were unwilling to utterly destroy them. But everything despised and worthless, that they utterly destroyed.
> —1 SAMUEL 15:7–9

The story continues with Samuel rising early the next morning and going out to meet Saul. When

King Saul approached Samuel, he said, "Blessed are you of the Lord! I have performed the commandment of the Lord" (v. 13). The prophet responded by wanting to know that if Saul indeed obeyed the command of the Lord, why did Samuel hear the sound of sheep

Insecure leaders are more concerned with developing the outward man than with developing the inward man.

and cattle. Saul replied by saying, "They have brought them from the Amalekites; for the people spared the best of the sheep and the oxen, to sacrifice to the Lord your God; and the rest we have utterly destroyed" (v. 15).

70

Notice whom Saul blames for this violation against God's command—"for the people…" Once again Saul is unwilling to take responsibility for his own sin and willing to sacrifice the people on the altar of his own personal ambition.

But Samuel sharply rebuked Saul, saying:

> "Be quiet! And I will tell you what the Lord said to me last night." And he [Saul] said to him, "Speak on." So Samuel said, "When you were little in your own eyes, were you not head of the tribes of Israel? And did not the Lord anoint you king over Israel? Now the Lord sent you on a mission, and said, 'Go, and utterly destroy the

sinners, the Amalekites, and fight against them until they are consumed.'"

—1 SAMUEL 15:16–18

Samuel gave Saul a second chance to take responsibility for his actions, asking Saul again, "Why then did you not obey the voice of the LORD? Why did you swoop down on the spoil, and do evil in the sight of the LORD?" (v. 19).

But Saul was insistent in his excuse and said, "But I have obeyed the voice of the LORD...But the people took the plunder, sheep and oxen, the best of the things which should have been utterly destroyed, to sacrifice to the LORD your God in Gilgal" (vv. 20–21).

Samuel proceeded to inform Saul that because he had rejected the word of the Lord, the Lord had rejected him as king. Saul immediately responded by saying, "I have sinned, for I have transgressed the commandment of the LORD and your words, because I feared the people and obeyed their voice" (v. 24).

Saul said the right words, but he lacked the sincerity of true repentance—evident from his next comment: "Now therefore, please pardon my sin, and return with me, that I may worship the LORD" (v. 25).

71

Samuel had just informed Saul that the hand of God had been lifted from him. In essence, Samuel was telling Saul that he would finish out his reign as king without the anointing of God. Yet Saul responded by asking Samuel to come and worship with him. In other words, Saul wanted Samuel to help him keep up appearances before the people, giving the illusion that God was still with him as king. Saul was more concerned with his own image than he was with the reality that he had lost the favor of God!

A spirit of insecurity always places more value on appearances than reality. Insecure leaders will spend time, energy and money to create an image that they think will secure their worth in the eyes of others. Insecure leaders are more concerned with developing the outward man than with developing the inward man.

It is only for a limited time that we can get by with such a superficial approach to life. In time, people will begin to recognize the thin veneer covering up who we really are. The issues of life have a way of ultimately exposing the true nature of the heart. If we would spend as much time building the inward man in humility and true dependence upon Jesus as we do carefully crafting the image of outward, we just might begin to experience full-blown revival.

TRAITS OF A SECURE LEADER

As we have discovered in this chapter, the traits of an insecure leader are a lust for the approval of man, cowardice, jealousy and a preoccupation with appearances. In the Scriptures we see an answer to each of these unhealthy traits as well as a clear description of the characteristics of a healthy, Christ-centered leader.

In Philippians 2:3–4 the apostle Paul confronts these unhealthy attitudes, saying, "Let nothing be done through selfish ambition or conceit, but in lowliness of mind let each esteem others better than himself. Let each of you look out not only for his own interests, but also for the interests of others."

I want to bring your attention to the word *conceit.* The word *conceit* in the Greek is *kenodoxia.* It describes someone who has an excessively high opinion of himself. This is someone who out of insecurity is fighting for a sense of personal worth. As a result, this person is so busy trying to establish his or her value that he or she loses sight of the value of others.

If we see our value in Christ, and understand that our worth is intrinsic, then we can afford to value and celebrate others. Our security in God's love gives us the freedom to esteem others better than ourselves. It is our security in God's love that liberates us from jealousy, cowardice and the need to keep up appearances for the approval of man.

Instead of being driven with the desire for the approval of man, we find ourselves living for the approval of God alone. Instead of being afraid of confrontation and honesty, the attitude of servanthood gives us the courage to deal openly and honestly with people. Instead of being jealous when we hear of the success of others, God's love empowers us to celebrate the success of others. It is the attitude expressed in Philippians 2:3–4 that sets us free from the need to keep up appearances to impress those around us.

A wonderful example of a leader who walks in the security of God is a friend of mine who pastors a large church in Oklahoma. While away from home, a couple in his church visited another church where missions was a very big part of the church's vision. After they returned home, they talked to the pastor about the impact that church's vision for missions had upon them. They wanted to know why their own church didn't have the same vision for missions.

The pastor explained to them that the church did give large sums of money each year to different mission projects and missionaries. Yet, even so, he didn't have any direction to redirect the activities of the church like the one this couple had visited. Each Sunday after the service, this couple would come down to the front and

73

ask the pastor if he had changed his mind, asking, "Why can't we be more like church so-and-so?"

Finally, after several weeks, the pastor said, "Listen, I love and respect the church you visited a few months ago. I love and respect the pastor; he is a personal friend of mine. But I am not him. I don't have the same vision for missions that he has. If you feel so strongly about his vision, maybe you should attend his church."

The man and his wife were startled by the pastor's straightforward honesty. Shortly after, they did leave the church. They didn't attend the church they had visited since it was in another state. They did, however, begin to attend a church in the same community that had a very strong vision for missions. My friend blessed them and prayed for them as they left.

Some time afterward my friend ran into this couple in a store. They embraced their former pastor and thanked him for all he had done in their lives. Then they informed him that they were on staff as the new missions directors of the neighboring church. My friend was genuinely glad for them. Because of this pastor's security in the Lord, he was able to truly rejoice with this couple and maintain a healthy, Christlike relationship with them.

I pray that there will be more pastors like this one who realize that the people belong to Jesus. They are His *sheep*, and as the Great Shepherd He has the right to lead His sheep to the pastures He has for them.

---

1. Stephen R. Covey, *Principle-Centered Leadership* (n.p., Summit Books, 1991).

QUESTIONS

Chapter 3
Traits of an Abusive Leader

1. Insecurity is a key root of abusive behavior. Explain how Saul allowed his desire for man's approval to destroy his relationship with God.

   _____

   _____

   _____

   _____

   _____

   _____

   _____

   _____

2. Explain how a spirit of insecurity causes us to place unwarranted value on appearance rather than reality.

   _____

   _____

   _____

   _____

   _____

   _____

   _____

   _____

   _____

   _____

3. Give an example from your own life (or from the life of a spiritual leader whom you respect) of a time when you responded to a circumstance out of your desire for Christ's approval rather than out of your desire for the approval of man.

_____

_____

_____

_____

_____

_____

_____

_____

_____

CHAPTER 4

TOXIC LOVE

WARNING:
SPIRITUAL ABUSE AHEAD

The idea of loyalty was not only the watchword in the services, but seemed to extend beyond the church, encroaching into their personal lives as well. For example, when another church in town had a special service, even if it didn't conflict with their services, it was considered a sign of disloyalty for anyone to attend from Pastor Doug's church.

John and Mary had been attending their local church for the last three years. Mary grew up in a healthy, Christian home. John, on the other hand, had a difficult childhood. First of all, his father's career kept him on the road a lot. When John's father was home, he constantly tore down John with his words. No matter how hard he tried, it seemed there was nothing John could do to earn his father's approval. Even though John was now in his mid-forties, his relationship with his father continued to be strained, and John continued to find himself desperately seeking the approval of those in authority.

When he and Mary first started to attend their church three years ago, it seemed to be the answer to their prayers. The people were friendly, and the services were exciting. John and Mary were especially impressed with the pastor of the church. Each Sunday John and Mary would sit in awe as they listened to his sermons. Pastor Doug was young, full of charisma and passionate about winning the lost. John and Mary were also impressed with the pastor's uncompromising message of commitment to Christ. For John, this was exactly the kind of man he felt he could follow.

It wasn't long before Pastor Doug began to reach out to John. John was excited with the idea of getting better acquainted with the pastor. He found himself filled with a fresh sense of importance. Even though John found it hard to believe that the pastor would want to take a special interest in him, he welcomed the attention.

It wasn't long before John found himself working closely with Pastor Doug. John really liked the idea of being a part of the "inner circle." The acceptance that he had desired for years and never received from his father had left an empty place in John's soul. Finally, John was receiving the approval he had always longed for.

Soon his responsibilities at the church demanded more and more of his time. It seemed that every night was taken up with a special meeting, church service or

For John and Mary, attending church had subtly become a way to earn the pastor's approval, a kind of "eye service" instead of a time of true worship and celebration.

project that needed to be done. John threw himself into his newly found responsibilities. John knew that he needed to work as unto the Lord, but with the completion of each task, John found himself looking for some sign of approval from the pastor. When John did receive any type of affirmation from Pastor Doug, he was left with a feeling of elation.

As time went on, John's involvement at the church began to put a strain on his and Mary's relationship. The more John gave, the more the pastor seemed to require. John and Mary discovered that the messages of commitment and loyalty they had initially heard and enjoyed were more than just an *emphasis* at the church—*they were the theme*. They also realized that the pastor's definition of commitment was different from theirs.

The idea of loyalty was not only the watchword in the services, but seemed to extend beyond the church, encroaching into their personal lives as well. For example, when another church in town had a special service,

80

even if it didn't conflict with their services, it was considered a sign of disloyalty for anyone to attend from Pastor Doug's church.

It also became apparent to John and Mary that the relationship people had with the church was placed on the same level as their relationship with Jesus. Folks were expected to be at church every time the doors were opened. If not, it was not only an indictment against their loyalty to Pastor Doug, but also toward God.

Ever since they first came to Christ, John and Mary knew that church attendance was important. Yet, for John and Mary, attending church had subtly become a way to earn the pastor's approval, a kind of "eye service" instead of a time of true worship and celebration.

Even though John recognized these danger signals, when Mary would place a demand on his time for something other than "church work," it usually resulted in a fight. These small skirmishes often escalated into all-out wars, filled with intense emotions and harsh words. These times of conflict ended with Mary in tears, begging John to slow down and invest more time in their marriage. John was frustrated because he couldn't understand why Mary didn't see how important his church responsibilities were. After all, they were building God's kingdom. What could be more important? Yet, as each month passed, Mary felt that she was losing more of John to the church.

Despite John seeing the obvious "red flags" in the church, as well as the impact his involvement was having on his marriage, he couldn't imagine backing off on his commitments. For the first time in his life, John was receiving the validation he always wanted and needed. Not only that, but John had seen firsthand how Pastor

81

Doug handled disappointment. Consequently, John couldn't stand the thought of his pastor's rejection.

It all came to a head when John came home from work one day to find a note on the kitchen table. It was from Mary. Simply put, she couldn't continue in the

Since the controllers aren't going to go away, we need to examine what gives them their power.

marriage the way it was. She had left for her mother's. She wasn't asking for a divorce. In fact, she affirmed her commitment to make the marriage work, but she felt there needed to be some significant changes—including that they find another church to attend. With her note, Mary included the name of a licensed Christian counselor located in town. Mary expressed her feeling that they needed some serious counseling, and she wanted John to initiate the first step by calling and making an appointment for both of them.

82

In a panic, John immediately called the pastor. It wasn't long before the pastor came to the house. John showed him the note, wanting to know what he should do. The pastor quickly explained that Mary was in rebellion to God because she wanted John to choose her over the church. "In addition," explained the pastor, "she is in sin for leaving." The pastor counseled John to draw a fast and hard line. "This is the time for tough love," the pastor concluded. John needed to demand that Mary return and *submit* to her husband and to the pastor's authority.

A still, small voice in John's heart told him that this was the wrong approach. But John feared the consequences if he disobeyed the pastor. Despite his good judgment, John handled the situation exactly as he was told and held his ground. Through the following year John refused to compromise his position. In one service, Pastor Doug even used John as an example from the pulpit of someone who really understands commitment and loyalty. John thinks back on that service with fondness, remembering how the people clapped and the pastor smiled approvingly. *It felt good to be so admired*, John mused as he drove home from another Sunday service.

Once home, John tossed his keys on the kitchen table and sorted through Saturday's mail. He hadn't had time to do it earlier; he was at the church all day Saturday and well into Saturday evening. In addition to the normal junk mail and bills, there was a manila envelope. John opened it, and the contents inside informed him that his divorce was final. John attempted to comfort himself with the thought, *Well, at least I'm not the one who sinned. It was Mary who filed.*

83

John is still a part of the inner circle there at his church. He sure enjoys his time there. Maybe it's because he hates walking into the silent, empty rooms of what was once a home.

This story is a compilation representing all too many lives in the body of Christ. Not only is it tragic, but it's also an abomination to all that is right and holy. We can shake our fists in anger at controlling pastors like Pastor Doug, but that would be futile. Sadly, controlling pastors are always going to be around. It reminds me of what Jesus commented concerning the poor: "The poor you have with you always..." Since the controllers aren't going to go away, we need to examine what gives them their power. Once we discover that, we can begin to free ourselves from the grip they have over our souls.

Their insecurity became so strong, and their desire for recognition became so intense, they were willing to pay any price to gain the validation of man!

In the previous chapter we looked at the attributes of the controlling pastor. In this chapter we need to look at what it is in people that allows them to be attracted to unhealthy churches.

In the last chapter we looked at the life of Saul. He wasn't alone in the abusive system that fed his insecurities. Israel was involved in creating the system that was able to empower Saul. As we look at the events surrounding Israel's desire for a king, we will discover where spiritual abuse begins, as well as how we can break its power over our lives.

THE INSECURITY OF A NATION

Israel first demanded that the prophet Samuel give them a king to rule over them in 1 Samuel 8. That chapter tells us the main reason for their demand:

> Then all the elders of Israel gathered together
> and came to Samuel at Ramah, and said to him,
> "Look, you are old, and your sons do not walk in

your ways. Now make us a king to judge us like
all the nations."

—1 Samuel 8:4–5

The people's request troubled Samuel's heart. Yet
Samuel took Israel's request to the Lord in prayer.
God responded to Israel's request with these words:

> Heed the voice of the people in all that they say
> to you; for they have not rejected you, but they
> have rejected Me, that I should not reign over
> them. According to all the works which they
> have done since the day that I brought them out
> up out of Egypt, even to this day—with which
> they have forsaken Me and served other gods—
> so they are doing to you also. Now therefore,
> heed their voice. However, you shall solemnly
> forewarn them, and show them the behavior of
> the king who will reign over them.

—1 Samuel 8:7–9

Within God's warning, He called Israel to remem-
brance of all He had done for them as their king. God
had accomplished for them what no earthly king could
ever accomplish. God reminded Israel of how supernatural their success and existence had been. God
made it clear to Samuel that Israel's desire for a king is
not a rejection of the prophet, but of God. In other
words, God is saying that Israel would rather have a
man rule them than God. God commanded Samuel to
warn Israel sternly of what the consequences would be
to have a king rule over them.

Years ago when I first read this verse, I thought God
was referring to Saul's subsequent reign over Israel
and was warning the people that Saul would be an evil

85

king. However, once I looked at the consequences that Samuel explained to Israel, I realized that there was nothing in them that represented sin on the part of *the king*. God was explaining how an earthly kingdom functions—no matter who is king.

In 1 Samuel 8:11–17, we see what Scripture calls the "behavior of the king":

> This will be the behavior of the king who will reign over you: He will take your sons and appoint them for his own chariots and to be his horsemen, and some will run before his chariots. He will appoint captains over his thousands and captains over his fifties, will set some to plow his ground and reap his harvest, and some to make weapons of war and equipment for his chariots.
>
> He will take your daughters to be perfumers, cooks, and bakers. And he will take the best of your fields, your vineyards, and your olive groves, and give them to his servants. He will take a tenth of your grain and your vintage, and give it to his officers and servants. And he will take your male servants, your female servants, your finest young men, and your donkeys, and put them to his work. He will take a tenth of your sheep. And you will be his servants.

In essence God warned Israel that by desiring an earthly king, they would forfeit an immense amount of rights and privileges they currently enjoyed. Many in Israel would see their families fractured. Sons and daughters would be taken from homes—for the rest of their lives. From this time on, the only time many in Israel would see their children was from a distance.

Scripture also declared that the best of Israel's vineyards and groves would go to the king's servants. The best of all the servants from Israel would be placed in service to the king. Thousands of husbands, fathers and sons would be drafted to serve in the king's army. Finally, the king would have the right to exact a tax of 10 percent of all the people's increase.

It is within the love of God that we discover our worth and value.

Interestingly, at the last minute, God tried to give Israel an opportunity to repent of their choice. God instructed Samuel to go over the list of consequences again—right before they crowned Saul as king. Israel's response was the same then as it had been when they first heard it.

Notice how Israel responded to Samuel's warning:

87

> Nevertheless the people refused to obey the voice of Samuel; and they said, "No, but we will have a king over us, that we also may be like all the nations, and that our king may judge us and go out before us and fight our battles."
> —1 Samuel 8:19–20

Israel's rationale for wanting a king was because Samuel hadn't done a good job raising his sons. They were not godly men, and since Samuel wasn't going to be around much longer, the people of Israel felt that they needed someone to rule them. But there was a deeper reason why they wanted a king. Verse 20 reveals their real reason for being so insistent on having a king: "...that we also may be like all the nations."

Israel had sensed the contempt from other nations surrounding them because they had no king. These other people groups had a king to whom they could point as their ruler. When an Israelite was asked by one of these heathen people who their king was, they would reply that it was Jehovah. Yet they couldn't describe Him physically, and they certainly couldn't see Him. As a result, the other nations didn't take Israel seriously. Eventually, this troubled the people of Israel to the point that they approached Samuel demanding that a king be set over them—just like the other nations.

Israel had become obsessed with winning the approval and acceptance of the other nations. They were even willing to give up their sons and daughters to secure this recognition. Israel was a supernatural people. They existed as a nation because of God. What separated them from the other nations was their covenant with God. Their identity and destiny were in Jehovah. Yet when Israel began to desire the approval of the other nations, they forgot all of this. Their insecurity became so strong, and their desire for recognition became so intense, they were willing to pay any price to gain the validation of man!

88

THE GREATEST LONGING OF THE HUMAN HEART

In my book *Life Without Fear,* I talk about how strong this kind of insecurity can be by using the example of the initiation rites of many street gangs.

> The fear of man is described as a snare because
> we actually become captured and imprisoned by

others in our need for their acceptance. We say and do things that we otherwise wouldn't do in order to gain the validation we feel we need. An extreme example of this is the initiation rites of some gangs. Many gangs require a prospective member to endure bloody beatings from the members before that person is accepted into the "fold." It is amazing that young men and women will endure these brutal attacks just for the acceptance of those in the gang and to gain a sense of identity as one of its members.[1]

Just as the Israelites were willing to pay any price to gain the approval of man, so these gang members were willing to pay this price. But the problem doesn't stop there—what happened with Israel happens to us individually as well. In the same way...

We subject ourselves to the same type of cruelty. With us, though, it is manifested in relationships that strip us of our dignity and individuality. Though not physical, this abuse occurs on a much deeper level than one gang member physically attacking another. The fear of man can grip us in continuing abusive or controlling relationships where we allow others to run our lives. We may even find ourselves willing to abandon our life purpose and to sacrifice our marriages and families—all in an attempt to be accepted.[2]

89

I am convinced that the greatest need of the human heart is the need to be loved and accepted. Though we are faced with many needs throughout our lives (healing, finances, guidance, strength, wisdom, restored relationships), no need surpasses this chief of all needs.

Though it may sound amazing, God created us with this need. It is a part of our makeup—our DNA, if you will. Therefore, the need for love and acceptance will never go away—it must be met. Because God placed that need within us, only He can completely satisfy our need for love. Another way of looking at it is this—God created us desperately needing who He is—Love!

It is within the love of God that we discover our worth and value. As a result, each day we instinctively find ourselves seeking to satisfy this primary yearning for acceptance. We are either looking to the Father to satisfy this longing for love, or we are looking to others. The moment we turn to others to meet that need, our souls become captured with a spirit of insecurity. When we allow the acceptance of others to determine our worth, we become slaves to the opinions and attitudes of those around us. We begin to live for the approval of man.

Jesus spoke of this insecurity in John 5:42–44, saying:

> But I know you, that you do not have the love of God in you. I have come in My Father's name, and you do not receive Me; if another comes in his own name, him you will receive. How can you believe, who receive honor from one another, and do not seek the honor that comes from the only God?

Jesus rebuked the Pharisees strongly for their selfish ambition. Pharisees live to gain the approval of men. The reason? Because they did not "have the love of God" within them. The Pharisees, like anyone else, had the need for love and acceptance. Not having a revelation of the love of God, they searched for worth in the acceptance of the people. Because they couldn't see how much God loved them, they defined their value by how man received them. Since the Pharisees' worth lay within the acceptance of the people, they constantly lived to impress others.

Jesus refers to the Pharisees' inability to discern truth by saying, "I have come in My Father's name, and you do not receive Me; if another comes in his

Within adult relationships, people control us only if we give them the power to do so.

own name, him you will receive" (v. 43). Even though Jesus came in the name of God Almighty, the religious leaders were unable to recognize Him. Yet, when someone else comes in his own authority, full of pride, the Pharisees quickly receive him.

I have often wondered why some people are unable to discern the motivations of certain preachers who clearly have their own agendas. I finally realized that the only way to make room for the ambitions of others is to do so within our own ambitions. By making room for someone who ministers for the approval of others, we secure a place to pursue our own agenda.

Jesus continues to say, "How can you believe, who receive honor from one another, and do not seek the honor that comes from the only God?" (v. 44). In other words, Jesus was saying, "How can you have a vibrant, fulfilling, intimate fellowship with God and look to others to satisfy the need for love?" It's a trade-off. Any time we look to others to meet our longing for acceptance, we sacrifice our intimacy with the only

91

One who can truly satisfy our soul's deepest desire—security in His love.

As long as we continue to look to others to satisfy our need for acceptance, we will be at risk for being controlled. In unhealthy churches, two dynamics are always at work. One, there needs to be the controller—someone who through his insecurities has a desperate need to be needed. Second, there are those who, out of their own insecurities, need the acceptance of someone whom they view as greater than them. Somehow, if we can get someone whom we perceive of greater worth to validate us, then we feel that it increases our worth as well.

Breaking the Power of the Controller

How do we break the power of a controlling pastor or spiritual leader? We find the answer by looking at the life of Jesus. Let me ask you this question: "Have you ever been controlled, or have you manipulated someone else?" In the thirty-three years of Jesus' life on earth, not one time was He ever controlled or manipulated. Why? Because He never gave anyone access to the place in His life where someone else had the power to control Him.

In John 2:23–25, we read:

> Now when He was in Jerusalem at the Passover, during the feast, many believed in His name when they saw the signs which He did. But Jesus did not commit Himself to them, because He knew all men, and had no need that anyone should testify of man, for he knew what was in man.

Jesus experienced a time of popularity in His ministry. The people were amazed and excited about the things He said and did. Yet Scripture says that Jesus did not commit Himself to them. It doesn't say that Jesus wasn't committed to them—but that He did not commit Himself to them. In other words, Jesus didn't allow their praise to take His focus off the love of the Father.

Jesus knew what could be in the hearts of men. He knew that people could throw down palm leaves and praise one minute, and be screaming for blood the next minute. We find the key to Jesus' resistance to control or manipulation in verse 25: Jesus "had no need that anyone should testify of man..."

Jesus didn't need the testimony of any man. He didn't need anyone's affirmation to convince others He was the Christ. More importantly, Jesus didn't need man's testimony to secure His sense of worth and value. Jesus wasn't insecure. Christ knew who He was regardless of the fact that others didn't. The reason Jesus didn't fall into the trap of being controlled by others was because He found fulfillment to His need to be loved and accepted *in the love of the Father.*

When Israel demanded a king, Samuel warned them of the following consequence: "And you will cry out in that day because of your king whom you have chosen for yourselves, and the LORD will not hear you in that day" (1 Sam. 8:18). That may seem harsh and uncompassionate, but we must understand what God is saying: "You may think this is what you need and that this is what is going to make you happy. But at some point there will be pain in this relationship."

I am sure that most of us can relate to that statement. It is painful to realize that we have been manipulated and taken advantage of. When the pain begins, our response is to cry out to God to make it stop, to vindicate us in some way. Yet God, in essence, is saying, "I didn't start it, so I can't stop it."

93

Like Israel, we have set someone other than God as a "king" in our hearts. We have enthroned the opinions and attitudes of others. And since we are the ones who empowered their influence in our lives, we are the only ones who can dis-empower them.

Within adult relationships, people control us only if we give them the power to do so. How do we empower the controller and manipulator over our lives? By allowing their words to carry more value than God's. When we look to others to determine our worth, then their opinions and attitudes carry more weight than God's opinion of us. Consequently we find ourselves trapped within their moods and words and living for their approval. If you or I have been controlled or manipulated in the past, it is only because we gave others the place and power to do so.

It's not too late. If you are reading these pages and are still reeling from a painful experience with an unhealthy church or a controlling leader, your freedom and healing can begin today. Instead of expending your energy in anger toward the abuser, take responsibility and admit to yourself that the power they had to control was the power you gave them. Release them in forgiveness, and turn toward your heavenly Father, allowing His love to bathe your soul. As it does, the power of His passion will bring healing and security as you discover your intrinsic worth and value in Him.

94

---

1. Mike Fehlauer, *Life Without Fear* (Lake Mary, FL: Charisma House, 2000), 83–84.
2. Ibid., 84.

QUESTIONS

Chapter 4
Toxic Love

1. Oftentimes people are drawn into abusive church situations because they have a strong desire for affirmation and attention from a leader. How can we overcome this tendency?

_____

_____

_____

_____

_____

_____

_____

2. Jesus understood the Father's love for Him, so He did not derive His worth from the attention or praise of men. How well do you feel you really know and understand the unconditional love of God?

_____

_____

_____

_____

_____

_____

_____

3. Read John 2:23–25. Why do you think Jesus never allowed a man to manipulate or control Him?

_____

_____

_____

_____

_____

_____

_____

_____

_____

_____

_____

_____

_____

_____

CHAPTER 5

"TOUCH NOT
MY ANOINTED"

WARNING:
SPIRITUAL ABUSE AHEAD

The pastor went on to say that since Sherry
had continued to see him, she was in
rebellion to his spiritual authority. He
further warned her that if she persisted in
her rebellion, he had no choice but to
remove her from every area of ministry
where she was serving within the church.

Sherry was actively involved in her church; she was there every time the doors opened. Attractive, single and a successful career woman, she had been introduced to a young man through a mutual friend. He was a strong Christian and attended a different church in town. Sherry began to date this young man and enjoyed his company. They spent most of their time talking about the things of the Lord.

At one point, Sherry's pastor discovered that she was dating this young gentleman. After one Sunday service, the pastor asked to see Sherry in his office. "I don't approve of you dating this young man," he informed Sherry. "He is not a member of our church."

Even though Sherry was troubled by her meeting with the pastor, she continued to see this young man. A few weeks later, the pastor had one of his associates call Sherry and schedule another meeting with him. Feeling intimidated, Sherry asked her mother, also a member of the church, to come with her as she met with the pastor.

The pastor was surprised and visibly agitated to see Sherry's mom with her. Both Sherry and her mom accompanied the pastor back to his office. He reminded Sherry that he had forbidden her to date this young man. The pastor went on to say that since Sherry had continued to see him, she was in rebellion to his spiritual authority. He further warned her that if she persisted in her rebellion, he had no choice but to remove her from every area of ministry where she was serving within the church.

Sherry just sat there in her chair as she endured the pastor's verbal tirade. With her head down in shame, tears slowly dropped from her long lashes and landed on the front of her blouse.

99

Finally, Sherry's mom spoke up. First she expressed to the pastor their family's love for him. Then she went on to say that they both felt it wasn't his place to dictate to Sherry whom she could date. That, respectfully speaking, was none of his business.

Controlling pastors believe they are to be obeyed simply because of the office they hold.

It was obvious this pastor was not accustomed to someone questioning his authority. He quickly stood up from his desk, signifying that the meeting was over. Within a couple of days, Sherry was informed that she was not allowed to serve in any area of ministry within the church. It was explained that her punishment would continue until she repented to the pastor for her rebellion. During his sermon on the following Sunday, the pastor spent most of his time angrily insisting that when people rebel against him, they are really rebelling against God. Thankfully, Sherry and her mom found another church in the area to attend. They now are both experiencing the joy of attending a healthy, life-giving church.

Controlling pastors believe they are to be obeyed simply because of the office they hold. They conveniently use scriptures like Hebrews 13:17, which says, "Obey those who rule over you, and be submissive, for they watch out for your souls."

When insecure leaders are challenged regarding any type of dishonesty or hypocrisy, they often quote

Psalm 105:15: "Do not touch My anointed ones, and do My prophets no harm." Because of their interpretation of this verse, many pastors and leaders claim to have some form of "diplomatic immunity" from the biblical standards to which the rest of the body of Christ is held.

This spirit of control is not new to our generation. It has been operating in religious leaders for thousands of years. The prophet Ezekiel boldly declared the Lord's rebuke concerning the religious leaders of his day, saying:

> The weak you have not strengthened, nor have you healed those who were sick, nor bound up the broken, nor brought back what was driven away, nor sought what was lost; but with force and cruelty you have ruled them.
>
> —EZEKIEL 34:4

God was accusing the spiritual leaders in Ezekiel's day of ignoring the needs of the people and of using their positions of authority to beat down the people of God with their own set of rules and regulations. God the Father describes the priests as *shepherds* who have selfishly neglected the needs of the sheep in order to satisfy their own needs. The word *cruelty* in this verse can also be translated "harshness." In other words, according to the Lord, it was with a strong harshness that the religious leaders beat down and abused the people of Israel.

The Book of Matthew records how Jesus viewed the people of His day.

> But when He saw the multitudes, He was moved with compassion for them, because they were

101

weary and scattered, like sheep having no shepherd.

—MATTHEW 9:36

The word *weary* is the Greek word *skullo*, and it literally means "to be harassed." Jesus saw the people as innocent sheep who were being harassed and abused by the Pharisees. Obviously what was happening in

In the New Covenant, it is those who demonstrate the truth of God in their lives who operate in the authority of God.

the time of Ezekiel was still going on in Jesus' day—and it is still happening today.

102

FALSE AUTHORITY

How did the religious leaders of Jesus' day get away with their abuse of power? The same question could be asked of many religious leaders today. Jesus gives us the answer in the Book of Matthew.

> Then Jesus spoke to the multitudes and to His disciples, saying: "The scribes and the Pharisees sit in Moses' seat. Therefore whatever they tell you to observe, that observe and do, but do not do according to their works; for they say, and do not do."
>
> —MATTHEW 23:1–3

Jesus said that the scribes and Pharisees sat in the seat of Moses. Jesus was not referring to a literal seat or chair. In using the word *seat*, Jesus was describing a place or position of authority. For example, when Bonnie and I were in college, she was the secretary for the chair of the music department. Of course, the "chair" was actually the individual who was the head of that department. The Greek word for *seat* is the word *kathedra*. The Latin language has taken this word and made a phrase out of it, which is *ex cathedra*, meaning "to speak out of a place of authority."

Jesus reveals a powerful observation in Matthew 23:1. Jesus is saying that the scribes and Pharisees had seated themselves in the seat of Moses. In other words, these men had taken this authority upon themselves—and had not allowed God to give it to them (if He chose to do so). Therefore, these men were operating in their own power—not a God-given power.

Keep in mind that this place of authority is referred to as *Moses' seat*. As we look at the life of Moses, it is clear that he didn't operate in his own authority. Moses' authority came as the result of his relationship with God. Moses had authority because he spoke exactly what God had spoken to him. Yet, despite this truth, the religious leaders of Jesus' day had taken upon themselves a position of power and claimed to be speaking for God.

How could this happen? In Israel the requirement for leadership involved three different criteria. First, to have a position of power or authority you had to be old. Second, you had to be a Hebrew. Third, you had to be a man. In other words, if you were a Gentile woman who walked in the wisdom of God and the power of the Spirit, you could never hold a place of leadership. If

103

you were a Hebrew young man, or a Gentile male, you could never hold a position of authority, regardless of your relationship with the Lord.

Notice that in the religious system of Jesus' day, all three criteria for holding a position of authority were *external.* It isn't much different today. How convenient this type of system is for the abusive leader. Pastors all across the country demand that their people bow in submission to their authority—simply because they are in charge.

With the advent of the church age and with the coming of the Holy Spirit, this religious system, which had previously held people in bondage, had now been destroyed! In Acts Peter quotes the prophet Joel, saying:

> And it shall come to pass in the last days, says God, that I will pour out of My Spirit on all flesh; your sons and your daughters shall prophesy, your young men shall see visions, your old men shall dream dreams. And on My menservants and on My maidservants I will pour out My Spirit in those days; and they shall prophesy.
>
> —Acts 2:17–18

104

In these verses, the Spirit of God was establishing a new basis of authority. It is not based on *age* ("your young men shall see visions"). It is not based on *gender* ("your sons and your daughters shall prophesy"). It is not based on *race* ("and on My menservants and on My maidservants I will pour out My Spirit"). In the New Covenant, it is those who demonstrate the truth of God in their lives who operate in the authority of God. In other words, the criteria for walking in true authority were changed from being *external* to being *internal.*

GOD'S BASIS FOR AUTHORITY

When Jesus came to the earth, He gave up His authority as God. Yet He won back that authority through His life and His finished work on the cross. The apostle Paul explains this fact as he challenges us to a life of submission to the will of God. In Philippians 2:5–9 we read:

> Let this mind be in you which was also in Christ Jesus, who, being in the form of God, did not consider it robbery to be equal with God, but made Himself of no reputation, taking the form of a bondservant, and coming in the likeness of men. And being found in appearance as a man, He humbled Himself and became obedient to the point of death, even the death of the cross. Therefore God also has highly exalted Him and given Him the name which is above every name.

The authority Jesus now holds as the head of the church was not bestowed upon Him because of His position as the Son of God, but because of His obedience to the will of the Father. Verse 9 of the above passage starts off with the word *Therefore*, referring to what Jesus accomplished through His obedience. In other words, Paul is saying that it was because of Jesus' obedience to the Father that He was given the name that is above every name.

When the apostle Paul was instructing a young pastor by the name of Timothy concerning who should have authority in the local church, Paul gave Timothy an extensive list of character traits that were necessary for a position of leadership:

> A bishop then must be blameless, the husband of

105

one wife, temperate, sober-minded, of good behavior, hospitable, able to teach; not given to wine, not violent, not greedy for money, but gentle, not quarrelsome, not covetous; one who rules his own house well, having his children in submission with all reverence (for if a man does not know how to rule his own house, how will he take care of the church of God?); not a novice, lest being puffed up with pride he fall into the same condemnation as the devil. Moreover he must have a good testimony among those who are outside, lest he fall into reproach and the snare of the devil.

—1 Timothy 3:2–7

All of the character traits mentioned in the above passage are expressions of one's relationship with the Lord. All of these traits assert the need for a pastor to live an ethical and moral life. According to this passage, truth proceeds genuine authority. Or it could be said that authority can never extend beyond truth. It is not a position or a title that gives one authority, but it is a life of truth and integrity. If someone needs to tell you he is in charge, he probably isn't.

If a pastor isn't operating in authority given to him by God, then he will feel the need to exert his own authority through position or title. Pastors who are emotionally immature, or who lack integrity and character, instinctively recognize their lack of genuine power to influence others. As a result, they will compensate for their deficiency by borrowing strength from external sources, like position, title, intellect, image or possessions. Some other sources from which they may attempt to leverage strength might be size, appearance, credentials, status symbols or even associations with other powerful people.

It is not a position or a title that gives one authority, but it is a life of truth and integrity.

Many extremely controlling pastors have a steady stream of well-known preachers who come through their church. Some of these pastors will have an influential minister behind their pulpit on the average of twice a month. Not only can this create the problem of the people in that church not really knowing "who" their church really is, but it also creates the dynamic of shared credibility. For example, those who are beginning to suspect that they may be in an abusive church are often left confused when they see a minister whom they admire behind the pulpit that belongs to an abusive pastor. A controlling pastor knows all too well that he is borrowing strength from his association with well-known preachers in order to maintain influence with his own congregation.

107

In his book *Principle-Centered Leadership*, Stephen Covey states that when we borrow strength from external sources we build weakness in ourselves as well as others. Mr. Covey explains that eventually a person who does this will build weakness in three places:

> First, he builds weakness in himself. Borrowing strength from position or authority reinforces

his own dependence upon external factors to get things done in the future.

Is there is a way to borrow strength without building weakness? Yes! By borrowing from what has been developed internally— character, honesty, integrity, love and truth.

Second, he builds weakness in other people. Others learn to act or react in terms of fear or conformity, thus stunting their own reasoning, freedom, growth, and internal discipline.

Third, he builds weakness in the relationship. It becomes strained. Fear replaces cooperation. Each person involved becomes a little more arbitrary, a little more agitated, a little more defensive. To win an argument or a contest, an emotionally immature person may use his strengths and abilities to back people into a corner. Even though he wins the argument, he loses. Everyone loses. His very strengths become his weakness.[1]

Covey goes on to write:

In fact, whenever we borrow strength from external sources, we must ask ourselves what happens to us when these things change or are no longer there? Obviously we remain stuck with the weaknesses we have developed in ourselves, in our

108

relationships, and in others. In fact, people who have the habit of borrowing strength will eventually lose influence with those they want most to impress. Their children may feel belittled and crushed, with little sense of worth, identity, or individuality. Their co-workers may become rebellious and strike back in their own way, often at the very things they treasured the most.[2]

Is there is a way to borrow strength without building weakness? Yes! By borrowing from what has been developed internally—character, honesty, integrity, love and truth. These things give us a strength that surpasses the constant change of the external.

AUTHENTIC AUTHORITY COMES FROM INTEGRITY IN LIFE AND DOCTRINE

When the apostle Paul encouraged others to follow him, it was based on his life's example as well as on his accuracy in teaching the Word of God.

In Paul's second letter to Timothy, the apostle encouraged Timothy to remain faithful during times of great adversity. Paul was not asking Timothy to remain faithful to him as the apostle, but to Christ and to the gospel. In 2 Timothy 1:13, Paul writes, "Hold fast to the pattern of sound words which you have heard from me, in faith and love which are in Christ Jesus." It wasn't Paul's teaching that Timothy was encouraged to hold on to, but actually the Word of God, which Paul had taught Timothy. In the Book of 2 Corinthians, Paul challenges the church at Corinth to recognize his authority. Yet Paul explains that his authority with the church lies in the accuracy and honesty with which he preached to them the gospel.

109

> But we have renounced the hidden things of shame, not walking in craftiness nor handling the word of God deceitfully, but by manifestation of the truth commending ourselves to every man's conscience in the sight of God.
>
> —2 CORINTHIANS 4:2

In 2 Timothy 3:10, Paul speaks not only of what he taught, but also of the life he lived: "But you have carefully followed my doctrine, manner of life, purpose, faith, longsuffering, love, perseverance..." It was Paul's manner of life and his teaching that gave him the authority to speak as an apostle. Consequently, in 1 Corinthians 11:1, Paul encourages the Christians at Corinth to imitate him as he imitates Christ.

The apostle Paul was careful to instruct Timothy that his authority would also rest, first of all, in how accurately he taught the Word of God. Paul exhorted young Timothy:

110

> Be diligent to present yourself approved to God, a worker who does not need to be ashamed, rightly dividing the word of truth.
>
> —2 TIMOTHY 2:15

The phrase "rightly dividing" uses the compound Greek word *orthotomeo*, which means "to make a straight cut, or to dissect." A perfect picture illustrating this definition would be one of a surgeon operating on his patient with skillful accuracy. Timothy was to teach the Word of God with this same accuracy so that he would walk in the authority of God.

Paul also taught Timothy that it was necessary for him to have integrity not only in doctrine, but also within his personal life.

Meditate on these things; give yourself entirely to them, that your progress may be evident to all. Take heed to yourself and to the doctrine. Continue in them, for in doing this you will save both yourself and those who hear you.

—1 Timothy 4:15–16

Throughout history many great men of God have taken the time to develop a life of personal integrity and character. And developing the inner man does indeed take time. The act of leading can be challenging. As a result, the temptation that faces many leaders is to secure quick results. Consequently, they short-cut the process necessary to establish the inner strength needed in the life of a leader. I can think of several churches ten years ago that were some of the largest churches in America. The pastors of many of those churches were men who were long on vision and energy and short on character and integrity. As a result, many of these men are either no longer in the ministry, or their churches no longer exist.

It is clear from the Word of God that what we are on the inside is what we will live out on the outside. God's desire is that the shepherds of His people lead from a place of inner strength that only comes through faithful obedience over the long haul. God is not going to measure the effectiveness of our lives based on how big our churches are, but rather on our faithfulness to His Word and to His people.

111

---

1. Covey, *Principle-Centered Leadership*.
2. Ibid.

Chapter 5
"Touch Not My Anointed"

1. Why is it unbiblical for a pastor or leader to say that rebellion against his counsel is equal to rebellion against God?

   _____

   _____

   _____

   _____

2. Read Hebrews 13:17. What does it mean to "be submissive" to church leaders? Does it mean we must obey everything they tell us to do?

   _____

   _____

   _____

   _____

3. Read Psalm 105:15. This verse is often twisted to imply that it is never correct to challenge a leader's position or to question his decision. What do you think the verse really means?

   _____

   _____

   _____

   _____

   _____

4. Is it possible that someone who holds a position in a ministry or church does not actually operate in true spiritual authority? How can this be?

_____

_____

_____

_____

_____

_____

5. Personal integrity in character and doctrine is the basis for true spiritual authority—not a charismatic personality, preaching skills, money, celebrity status or clerical position. Explain this in the light of 2 Corinthians 4:2.

_____

_____

_____

_____

_____

_____

_____

_____

_____

HOW TO
RELATE TO YOUR
PASTOR

WARNING:
SPIRITUAL ABUSE AHEAD

The pastor thought it was his duty to humble the worship leader, so he asked some of the members of the church to put together a skit to be performed on a Sunday morning. The skit would, of course, center around the story of a worship leader who was walking in pride and needed to be brought down a few pegs.

One pastor of a small church decided that the volunteer worship leader had areas of pride in his life. The pastor thought it was his duty to humble the worship leader, so he asked some of the members of the church to put together a skit to be performed on a Sunday morning. The skit would, of course, center around the story of a worship leader who was walking in pride and needed to be brought down a few pegs.

The pastor wanted to be sure that the worship leader's wife would not be in the service that Sunday. As a result, a church staff member told her that she was needed in the nursery.

As the people performed their skit, it became clear to everyone whom the skit was about. Yet, in case there were any questions, at the conclusion of the skit the pastor called the worship leader to the front of the church and rebuked him publicly for his pride and arrogance.

This is another sad example of a pastor who didn't understand his role as a spiritual leader, resulting in spiritual abuse. In chapter 3 we looked at the traits of an abusive pastor. In this chapter I want to point out the characteristics of a healthy pastor. It is important to understand that just as the perfect church doesn't exist, neither does the perfect pastor. The church is made up of fallible human beings. Likewise, the church is also governed by fallible pastors. The issue is not how flawlessly a pastor discharges his or her duties. Instead, it is more an issue of the honesty and humility with which a pastor shepherds God's people.

As we look to the Scriptures, we see a picture of the standard to which God intends each pastor to strive in the life of a congregation. First Peter 5:1–4 gives us an extensive account of the role of a pastor, using the example of the apostle Peter, who functioned as the pastor over the church in Jerusalem. Peter shares what he has learned about the role of a pastor from observing firsthand the Great Shepherd.

> The elders who are among you I exhort, I who am a fellow elder and a witness of the sufferings of Christ, and also a partaker of the glory that will be revealed: Shepherd ["feed," KJV] the flock of God which is among you, serving as overseers, not by compulsion but willingly, not for dishonest gain but eagerly; nor as being lords over those entrusted to you, but being examples to the flock; and when the Chief Shepherd appears, you will receive the crown of glory that does not fade away.

A Picture of a Healthy Pastor

In verse 1, Peter addresses his exhortation to the elders. The word *elder* in the Greek is *presbus*, which is literally translated "ambassador." An *ambassador* is an individual who has been assigned to represent and extend the good will of someone greater than himself. The word *presbus* is where we get our English word *presbytery*, which carries the idea of oversight. It was commonly used to refer to those in a local church who had the responsibility of governing the spiritual direction and health of that local body. As we look at this passage in its context, Peter is clearly using the word *elder* to refer to the different pastors who are messengers of the Chief Shepherd, sent to represent and extend the good will of the Father, providing oversight to specific congregations throughout the region.

118

A PASTOR'S RESPONSIBILITY TO THE PEOPLE

"FEED THE FLOCK OF GOD..."

The first characteristic of a healthy pastor that we see in this passage is found in the first part of verse 2, which

> # The issue is not how flawlessly a pastor discharges his or her duties. Instead, it is more an issue of the honesty and humility with which a pastor shepherds God's people.

says, "Feed the flock of God" (KJV). The word *feed* is the Greek word *poimaino.* This word involves more than just a shepherd's technically feeding his sheep. It implies fulfilling all the duties of the shepherd—guiding, guarding and protecting the flock. Therefore, when applied to the pastor of a church, "feed the flock" refers to more than just the pastor preaching good sermons. It is a command, as a shepherd of God's flock, to guide, protect and lead the people to the "green pastures" of their relationship with Christ—to "shepherd" the flock. This involves watching over the spiritual atmosphere of the congregation to insure that it remains Christ-centered. It is also a command to offer the kind of guidance that protects the people from excesses, which distract the sheep from living within the lordship of the Chief Shepherd.

119

In the Gospel of John we read where Jesus instructs Peter personally in what would be his primary role as a pastor.

> So when they had eaten breakfast, Jesus said to Simon Peter, "Simon, son of Jonah, do you love Me more than these?"
>
> He said to Him, "Yes, Lord; You know that I love You."
>
> He said to him, "Feed My lambs."
>
> He said to him again a second time, "Simon, son of Jonah, do you love Me?"
>
> He said to Him, "Yes, Lord; You know that I love You."
>
> He said to him, "Tend My sheep."
>
> He said to him the third time, "Simon, son of Jonah, do you love Me?" Peter was grieved because He said to him the third time, "Do you love Me?"
>
> And he said to Him, "Lord, You know all things; You know that I love You."
>
> Jesus said to him, "Feed My sheep."
>
> —JOHN 21:15–17

120

In verse 15, when Jesus asked Peter to "feed My lambs," that word *feed* is a different word in the Greek than what we have previously looked at. The word *feed* in this verse is the Greek word *bosko*. This word means literally "to feed someone food." To be more specific, it means to spoon-feed them.

It is important to notice that Jesus uses the word *lamb*, which is a baby sheep. For example, when a human newborn becomes hungry, the baby does not have the ability to feed himself. That infant requires his mother to feed him. In the same way, Jesus is saying a primary role of a pastor is to make sure that newborn Christians are given an opportunity to discover and learn the essential basics of the Christian life.

Jesus challenged Peter to "tend My sheep." The word *tend* is the same Greek word translated "feed" that we saw in 1 Peter 5:2. In 1 Peter 5:2 that same word refers to fulfilling the entire office of a shepherd. In John 21:15 Jesus used this word in reference to sheep—adult lambs. The complete thought conveys the meaning that a primary role of a pastor is to provide the atmosphere and leadership necessary to bring young Christians to the place of maturity in Christ (lambs who are becoming sheep). This is what Jesus meant when He said, "Go therefore, and make disciples of all the nations" (Matt. 28:19). Disciples are more than just converts—they are immature Christians who are growing to the place of spiritual maturity.

"BE OVERSEERS..."

Another characteristic of a healthy pastor is one who provides mature spiritual oversight within the local church. In 1 Peter 5:2 we read, ""Shepherd [feed] the flock of God which is among you, serving as overseers." The word *overseers* is the Greek word *episkopeo*, which is translated as "elder." One fundamental idea of an overseer is one of responsibility. For example, in the Book of Revelation, we see Jesus bringing correction to the seven churches in Asia. Each time Jesus addressed one of the seven churches, He used the phrase "And to the angel to the church..." The word *angel* is the Greek word *aggelos*, which literally means "messenger." *Aggelos* is a name that speaks an office. It refers to a human messenger, specifically a bishop or presiding elder over a church.

121

When Jesus needed to bring correction to a congregation, He addressed the pastor of the church. It was the pastor who was ultimately held responsible for the spiritual health of the church—not the congregation.

Jesus is saying a primary role of a pastor is to make sure that newborn Christians are given an opportunity to discover and learn the essential basics of the Christian life.

Many pastors believe that the chief problem in the church today is rebellion on the part of the people. It seems as if we have wanted to hold the congregation responsible for the church's overall spiritual condition. As we look at the Scriptures, it is clear that it is the pastor that has the authority to change the spiritual climate of the church. Therefore, Jesus ultimately holds the pastor responsible, not the people.

Please don't misunderstand me—each individual within the congregation is responsible for his or her own relationship with Jesus. But when it comes to the church as a whole, it is the pastor who is challenged to provide the kind of leadership that will create a spiritual climate that will inspire the people in their relationship with God.

Often, as leaders, we find ourselves complaining about how the people in our churches don't give

122

enough or serve enough. We find it easy to complain and blame the people for their lack of commitment to Christ. We need to remind ourselves that our job as leaders is not to complain, but to lead! Jesus described the people as sheep. He was not making a comment on the spiritual I.Q. of the people, since sheep are the dumbest animals with four legs. Jesus described us as sheep because sheep need a shepherd. The people of our congregations, like sheep, will follow the direction of the quality of leadership we provide them. Instead of beating them into submission, we need to lead them to obedience to Christ.

"NOT BY CONSTRAINT ... "

First Peter 5:2 continues by saying that healthy pastors should shepherd the people—not out of compulsion, but willingly. The King James Version uses the word *constraint*. The Greek word for *constraint* is the word *anagkastos*. It means "to be forced to do something against natural feelings." In other words, we don't want to find ourselves pastoring with a resentful attitude toward God's people.

123

We can't afford to pastor our congregations just out of obligation. If we find ourselves leading out of a sense of obligation, it is because we have lost our sense of stewardship. We don't own anything—not even the people. Unless we minister out of a sense of servanthood, we may talk the language of servanthood, but we will eventually find ourselves resenting the demands that others make on our lives.

Naturally, there will be times when we don't feel like preaching or loving the people. But according to Scripture, we need to have a true heart desire for what we are doing. If we don't, then we either need to reexamine our calling or ask God to change our perspective. (Or it could mean that we desperately need a vacation.)

Any time money becomes the driving source behind a church or ministry, there is going to be manipulation and abuse.

"NOT FOR DISHONEST GAIN..."

In 1 Peter 5:2, the apostle declares that pastors are to shepherd the flock without any desire for "dishonest gain." The King James Version uses the phrase "filthy lucre." In other words, ministers of the gospel must not be driven by the love of money. In 1 Timothy 6:5 we read, "...useless wranglings of men of corrupt minds and destitute of the truth, who suppose that godliness is a means of gain. From such withdraw yourself."

124

The apostle Paul is warning us that there are those in leadership who see the church as a way for them personally to gain financially. Instead of empowering people by helping them to see the importance of financial stewardship, these men see people simply as a financial resource. Instead of looking at what we as leaders can do to impart life in others, we find ourselves looking to the people in terms of what they can financially do for us.

For example, one church in the South demands that every member provide a statement of their annual income so they can check to see if the members are tithing. If they are found not tithing, then they are called in and threatened to obey the Word and tithe, or suffer God's wrath and destruction. I recently read of a church that sent a statement to members who had not tithed, warning them that they would be kicked out of the church if they didn't bring the giving of their tithes current.

Another pastor, after discovering how wealthy one couple in his church was, explained to them that it was his spiritual duty to instruct them regarding where they were to give their offerings, as well as how much to give and to whom. Any time money becomes the driving source behind a church or ministry, there is going to be manipulation and abuse.

"Nor as being lords..."

In 1 Peter 5:3 we read, "Nor as being lords over those entrusted to you, but being examples to the flock." The phrase "being lords over" is actually one word in the Greek language, which is the word *katakurieuo*. This word is actually a compound of two different Greek words. The first part of *katakurieo* is the word *kata*, which is literally translated into the phrase "down upon." This word signifies motion forcefully coming down from a higher place to a lower place. The second word is the Greek word *kurieuo*. This word means "to rule, to have dominion over, to exercise lordship over." These two words joined together create the phrase "being lords over."

Based on the definition of these words, another way the phrase "being lords over" can be described is "using a position of higher rank or privilege in order to exercise dominion over someone else, bearing down on them with a constant attitude of superiority."

125

The apostle Peter clearly commanded that pastors were to refrain from using their position of spiritual authority to exercise dominion over the people whom

God has divinely chosen pastors all over the world to love and lead the people to a place of victory life in Christ.

God has entrusted to them. In chapter 5 of this book we discussed in detail the boundaries of a pastor's spiritual authority in the lives of the people. The healthy pastor's attitude toward the people must be one of servanthood—not one of dominance. Because spiritual leaders have exercised their authority beyond the boundaries of God's Word, we have seen people become disciples of men, rather than disciples of Jesus.

"Those entrusted to you..."

Also, in 1 Peter 5:3 we read, "...over those entrusted to you." In the King James Version, the phrase "those entrusted to you" is translated as "God's heritage." The word *heritage* in the Greek is the word *kleros*, which is the same as our word *lot*. The word *lot* in this context refers to a stone that has been marked for the purpose of determining God's choice for a specific assignment or task.

For example, in biblical times, if people were having difficulty in determining God's choice for an assignment, they would cast lots. This was done by selecting a number of small stones that would represent the individuals involved in the selection process. Each stone was marked differently, representing each different individual. The stones were then placed in an urn. The urn was then shaken violently until the stones began to spill out. The first stone that fell to the ground was examined to determine which mark it contained. Depending on whose mark was found on the stone, it was then accepted that the "lot" had divinely fallen to that individual.

Of course, in this dispensation we have the Holy Spirit living within us; therefore, we don't need to cast lots in order to determine the will of God. We are able to follow the leadership of the Holy Spirit. The apostle Peter is not advocating that we go back to casting lots to determine the will of God. The point the apostle is making to the pastors whom he is addressing is that the "lot" has fallen to them to lead their respective congregations. God has divinely chosen pastors all over the world to love and lead the people to a place of victory life in Christ. Consequently, the apostle Peter is encouraging pastors to shepherd their congregations with a sense of divine purpose!

127

This verse is also a reminder that the people belong to the Lord. He is the one who has purchased them with His own blood. In Acts 20:28 we read, "Therefore take heed to yourselves and to all the flock, among which the Holy Spirit has made you overseers, to shepherd the church of God which He purchased with His own blood."

Notice this verse uses the phrase "the church of God." It is God's church. It was with His own blood that He purchased us. As pastors, it is important for us to remember that the people in our congregations belong to Him. For example, if there are folks who are causing problems, it is ultimately God's problem. No pastor has nail prints in his hands. We are merely stewards, chosen by God to love, lead and represent Him. We can't afford to take on the care of shepherding God's people, nor can we afford to be possessive of them.

"Be examples..."

First Peter 5:3 says, "...being examples to the flock." In 1 Corinthians 11:1, the apostle Paul said, "Imitate me, just as I also imitate Christ." Paul lived his life in such a way that he could, with confidence, challenge the Corinthian church to follow his example in living for Christ. Paul described his life to the Corinthians with these words:

> For our boasting is this: the testimony of our conscience that we conducted ourselves in the world in simplicity and godly sincerity, not with fleshly wisdom but by the grace of God, and more abundantly toward you.
>
> —2 Corinthians 1:12

128

Paul said that the example he set before them was, first of all, one of a life of simplicity. The word *simplicity* actually means a life of transparency. Paul is declaring that he lived his life void of any secrets or hidden agendas. Paul's life was an open book. When writing to his young friend Timothy, Paul said this about his life:

> But you have carefully followed my doctrine, manner of life, purpose, faith, longsuffering, love, perseverance, persecutions, afflictions, which happened to me at Antioch, at Iconium, at Lystra—what persecutions I endured. And out of them all the Lord delivered me.
>
> —2 Timothy 3:10–11

The apostle Paul's life was one that demonstrated trust in Christ and a sincere desire to serve others.

No pastor is perfect. Every pastor will make mistakes in judgment and direction. Yet the Scriptures are clear concerning the heart and attitude with which a

We need to recognize that pastors who are spiritually healthy and walking in their God-given authority are gifts from Jesus to enrich our lives and spiritual development.

pastor shepherds the flock of God. It is important that we understand the traits of a healthy pastor and recognize his heart of sincerity. It is only then that we can extend mercy and grace toward our pastors as they faithfully minister to us.

129

THE CONGREGATION'S RESPONSIBILITY TO THE PASTOR

Just as a pastor has specific responsibilities to the people over whom God has placed him in leadership, there are also responsibilities his people have to him. We will take a closer look at some of these responsibilities in this section.

RECOGNIZE THEM

The first responsibility that the congregation has to

the pastor is to recognize him. First Thessalonians 5:12–13 reads:

> And we urge you, brethren, to recognize those who labor among you, and are over you in the Lord and admonish you, and to esteem them very highly in love for their work's sake. Be at peace among yourselves.

The word *recognize* means "to perceive or acknowledge." In other words, the apostle Paul is saying that, first of all, we are to perceive and acknowledge the pastor as a gift to our lives. Ephesians 4:8 tells us, "When He [Jesus] ascended on high, He led captivity captive, and gave gifts to men." The word *gift* is the Greek word *doma*. Literally, it refers to the giving of a gift. Yet under close examination, this word speaks more of the quality of the gift than the benevolence involved in the giving of it.

In Ephesians 4:11 the apostle Paul describes the specific gifts Jesus has given to us, saying, "And He Himself gave some to be apostles, some prophets, some evangelists, and some pastors and teachers."

130

Clearly, the gifts that Jesus has given to us are the different ministry offices mentioned in verse 11. One of those offices is the office of the pastor. As we look at the gift of pastor in light of 1 Thessalonians 5:12, we see that we are to acknowledge the quality of the gift that lies within the life of our pastor. We need to recognize that pastors who are spiritually healthy and walking in their God-given authority are gifts from Jesus to enrich our lives and spiritual development.

ESTEEM THEM

We are admonished by the Word of God to "esteem

them [pastors] very highly in love for their work's sake" (1 Thess. 5:13). The word *esteem* is the Greek word *hegeomai*, which in this verse means "to reckon or to think."

It is amazing how the Lord provides for the needs of the church when they decide to obey the Scriptures and count their pastor worthy of double honor.

In other words, we are to think very highly of and respect greatly those who are over us in the Lord. It is the pastor who labors to teach us the Word of God, leading us in the path of life and peace. The Word admonishes us to esteem them highly "for their work's sake." You may not like certain aspects of your pastor's personality. You definitely will not always agree with him. Yet, despite these differences, we are to respect the position the pastor has in our lives.

131

HONOR THEM

We should honor our pastors. In 1 Timothy 5:17 we are advised, "Let the elders who rule well be counted worthy of double honor, especially those who labor in the word and doctrine."

The word *honor* is the Greek word *time*, pronounced *tee-may*. It means "money paid." This is consistent with what Paul is saying in this passage, as we read in the following verse: "For the scripture says, 'You shall not muzzle an ox while it treads out the grain,' and, 'The laborer is worthy of his wages'" (v. 18).

Here the apostle Paul is dealing with the way a pastor is to be financially compensated for his work in the ministry. This scripture says that those pastors who are ruling or leading well (who are living honestly and morally) are worthy of double honor— or double wages. Traditional thinking has been opposed to pastors and leaders being paid well. By and large, the position of pastor is one of the lowest-paid professions.

According to this scripture, it shouldn't be the pastor's responsibility to make sure that he is paid well and that his family is taken care of. It is the church's responsibility to make sure that he is being "honored." For years churches have felt it was their job to keep the pastor poor while the Lord kept him humble. The Word of God clearly teaches that the pastor is Jesus' gift to us, and it is the pastor who leads us in our development as Christians. Therefore, how we financially compensate the pastor communicates the value we place on our own spiritual lives. If we want to receive the benefit of what our pastor has to offer us spiritually, then we need to make sure that he is well paid.

132

There are several books that have been published showing the national averages for salaries paid to senior pastors and church staff based on the size and income of the church. My suggestion would be that each church board secure a copy of a compensation book, find the category into which they fit and then increase the senior pastor's salary by at least 10 percent. If the church is large and has associate pastors, then the same rule of thumb would apply to them as well. If a church isn't able to do that for the entire staff, then they should at least start by increasing the salary of the senior pastor. If the church has multiple staff, I would suggest it target, through faith and prayer, the increase of the salaries for the rest of the pastoral staff as soon as possible.

A healthy pastor will see himself as one who leads people to Jesus—the true Lifter of burdens.

The mistake that many churches make is to wait until they have an excess of undesignated funds lying around before they give the pastor a raise. First of all, a church is a nonprofit organization. It should never be the goal of a church to see how much money they have left at the end of a year. If a church does have excess money at the end of the year, that church probably wasn't doing much, or at least enough, to build the kingdom throughout the year.

133

Some churches may argue that they can't afford to pay their pastor well. I am saying that you can't afford not to pay your pastor well! It is amazing how the Lord provides for the needs of the church when they decide to obey the Scriptures and count their pastor worthy of double honor.

OBEY THEM—AND BE SUBMISSIVE

We are challenged to obey our spiritual leadership. In Hebrews we read:

> Obey those who rule over you, and be submissive, for they watch out for your souls, as those

who must give account. Let them do so with joy and not with grief, for that would be unprofitable for you.

—Hebrews 13:17

The main purpose of this book has been to identify what is biblical obedience and submission to spiritual authority. Here we see that the writer of Hebrews says we are to obey our spiritual authorities. It appears that this verse gives those in spiritual leadership an unquestioned authority over our lives. As a matter of fact, there have been many pastors who have used this verse to justify a despotic approach in dealing with people.

Let's take a closer look at the word *obey* here in Hebrews 13:17. The Greek word for *obey* is *peitho*, which means "to yield or to comply." This scripture is saying that we are to comply and yield to those in spiritual leadership. Yet, this is not an unqualified obedience. In other words, the Scriptures are not commanding us to obey someone just because they simply stand in the office of a pastor. Hebrews 13:7 provides a clear understanding of how and where we are to obey those in spiritual leadership over us:

134

> Remember those who rule over you, who have spoken the word of God to you, whose faith follow, considering the outcome of their conduct.

From this verse we can see that there are two major qualifications necessary in the life of a pastor before we are expected to obey him: "Remember those *who rule over you*, who have *spoken the word of God to you*" (emphasis added).

I want to bring your attention to the phrase "who have spoken the word of God to you." We are expected to obey only the Word of God. When faced with the question of obedience to a spiritual leader, the question should be asked, "Is the leader asking me to obey the Word of God or his own word?" The abusive leader will usually use Scripture to manipulate or control. Therefore we must carefully examine why a scripture is being used. The key to recognizing manipulation is determining whether we are being asked to obey a man or Jesus. It must be determined if the pastor is trying to use his influence to draw us toward himself or toward Jesus.

The phrase in that verse, "whose faith follow," speaks of the lifestyle of the leader. The question must be asked of every leader, "Does he live what he preaches—or does he preach what he practices?" Often controlling leaders play by a different set of rules than everybody else. Some believe they are exempt, above the law so to speak. They place requirements on others that they themselves have no intention of living under.

135

Jesus placed the Pharisees in this category of leadership. In Matthew 23:4, in speaking of the Pharisees, Jesus says, "For they bind heavy burdens, hard to bear, and lay them on men's shoulders; but they themselves will not move them with one of their fingers." The Pharisees controlled the people by weighing them down with rules that served their own personal agendas. A healthy pastor will see himself as one who leads people to Jesus—the true Lifter of burdens. This type of pastor will, through a life of integrity and compassion, lead others to a place of personal freedom and liberty.

In Summary

The Word of God clearly instructs us in how we are to relate to those who have a place of spiritual authority in our lives. How we relate to a pastor will determine the spiritual health of our lives and homes. We should *recognize* that our pastors are a gift to us from God to help establish and strengthen our lives. As we recognize this, we will learn to esteem them and to *value* and *honor* the gift of the pastor. The value we place on something determines the way we treat it.

Relating to a pastor in a healthy way would be incomplete if we didn't *obey* the teaching of God's Word. Jesus describes two different men who built a house. One built his house on a rock. As a result, when a violent storm came, his house continued to stand. Another man built his house on the sand. Consequently, when the storm came, because the foundation was weak, his house collapsed. Jesus said the difference between the two men was that the man who built his house on the rock was someone who heard and obeyed the Word of God. (See Matthew 7:24–29.) In the same way, it is not enough for us to hear truth— we must yield and obey the truth in order to withstand the storms of life.

Don't allow abusive leaders to poison your heart and cause you to become cynical. For every abusive pastor there are thousands of others who are honest and sincere. God has a pastor for you. God has a church for you. Trust Him to direct you to the church He desires for you. Expect Him to lead you in the path of righteousness and peace.

136

Chapter 6
How to Relate to Your Pastor

1. One requirement of a true shepherd is that he or she be able to "feed God's flock." Think of a pastor you have known, past or present, who faithfully carried out this duty. What are your fondest memories of this person's ministry?

_____

_____

_____

_____

2. Is it possible for pastors to lead their congregations without using force or constraint? How?

_____

_____

_____

_____

3. The New Testament tells church leaders to flee from the desire for "dishonest gain." What do you think are the warning signs of a church leader who is motivated by greed?

_____

_____

_____

_____

_____

QUESTIONS

4. The Word of God rebukes leaders who display an authoritarian attitude. Why do you think we find this attitude to be so common when it is condemned in the Bible?

_____

_____

_____

_____

5. Everyone makes mistakes, and leaders are no exception. Can you think of a time when someone in spiritual authority over you apologized for a mistake they made?

_____

_____

_____

_____

6. How would you describe your biblical responsibility to your pastor?

_____

_____

_____

_____

_____

_____

BREAKING TIES WITH THE ABUSIVE SYSTEM

WARNING:
SPIRITUAL ABUSE AHEAD

For years, Bob and Maria had noticed the sermons increasingly departing from the food of the Word to angry discourses of how people had let the pastor down. He would often tell horror stories of those who had left without his blessing, only sometime later to find themselves meeting with death or destruction.

The angry words pronouncing their curse rang loud in Bob and Maria's ears. They sat and wept quietly in their car as they drove home from the Sunday service. Neither one said anything as they both tried to make sense of what had just happened.

For years, Bob and Maria had noticed the sermons increasingly departing from the food of the Word to angry discourses of how people had let the pastor down. As a result, each Sunday more families were noticeably absent. Many Sundays the pastor threatened the congregation that if any more decided to leave, Satan himself would wreak havoc in their lives. He would often tell horror stories of those who had left without his blessing, only sometime later to find themselves meeting with death or destruction.

On one particular Sunday, he was on a rampage again. Bob and Maria decided they couldn't take the venom of hatred any longer. They got up to leave. Although there were nearly one thousand people in attendance, somehow Bob and Maria caught the attention of the pastor. Angrily, he called out, "If anyone wants to leave, go ahead! There's the door. The door won't get you on the way out, but the devil will!"

Bob and Maria were approaching the door to the sanctuary when they heard the threat. The words cut deep in their hearts. They had attended the church for years. They both had served faithfully in different areas of ministry, as well as giving thousands of dollars over the years. Bob and Maria had a lot invested in the church. Therefore, leaving wasn't an easy decision. As a matter of fact, they would later discover that it was the hardest decision they would ever make. All their friends were there. They knew from observing those who had

141

previously left that they too would be quickly ostracized. Neither Bob nor Maria were looking forward to what they would face—but they both knew that for the sake of their own spiritual lives, and their children's, there was no other choice.

As we have mentioned earlier in this book, a common belief in controlling churches is that there is no biblical reason for anyone to ever leave a church—unless, that is, they receive the pastor's blessing to do so. However, the problem is that a controlling pastor will be too insecure to render his blessing to anyone who leaves his "flock." If anyone does leave, they immediately become "the problem."

Consequently, those who do leave invariably will do so without the controlling leader's blessing. The situation becomes a double-edged sword. Those who do leave such an unhealthy or abusive church do so without the blessing of the insecure pastor. Consequently, they find themselves in rebellion to the pastor, which means they are in rebellion to God and therefore "in sin." Those who depart from an abusive church are usually considered to be backslidden, even if they go on to become actively involved in another church. *The sad truth is this: When leaving a controlling church, it is impossible to leave correctly in the eyes of the abusive pastor.*

If you find yourself needing to leave an abusive and controlling church, you need to realize that many times it will bring on attacks against your character. If you discover that you are in an abusive or unhealthy church and must make the decision to leave, it will be one of the most difficult challenges you will ever face. How you leave will determine and affect the condition of your heart. For example, leaving in anger will greatly hinder the healing process in your own life.

142

HOW TO LEAVE
AN ABUSIVE SITUATION

When breaking ties with an unhealthy church, there are several guidelines that I believe will help insure

> **When leaving a controlling church, it is impossible to leave correctly in the eyes of the abusive pastor.**

that your departure doesn't hinder you in receiving God's grace and healing.

1. GUARD YOUR HEART FROM UNFORGIVENESS.

> Keep your heart with all diligence, for out of it spring the issues of life.
>
> —PROVERBS 4:23

Because of the intensity of a controlling environment, and the fact that the issues of control deeply touch our sense of identity and worth, we face the danger of our hearts becoming poisoned with unforgiveness and anger. Before we make a decision to leave, it is extremely important that we examine our hearts. Anger, bitterness and unforgiveness can cloud our judgment and perception. We can find ourselves saying things and doing things that we will later regret.

As difficult as it might be to understand, the issue of forgiveness has nothing to do with the offender. It is an internal issue between God and us. I am convinced that the reason most believers have difficulty forgiving

143

is not due to a spirit of rebellion, but rather it is due to misunderstandings concerning what forgiveness is and how it is achieved.

One primary misconception concerning forgiveness is our wrong assumption that by forgiving someone, in essence we are ignoring the fact that any wrongdoing has taken place. Therefore if we believe this concept about forgiveness, then we may feel that forgiving the controlling leader requires that we ignore the abuse that took place—sort of pretending that it never happened. On the contrary, in order for true forgiveness to take place, honestly is *required*. There must be recognition of the wrong that has been done.

Forgiveness doesn't involve pretending that the offense never happened; it requires us to take responsibility for our response in light of the offense. Forgiveness begins when we realize that, indeed, we do have a choice. We can choose how we will respond to the abuser. We are not victims.

When we understand that forgiveness doesn't involve ignoring the offense, and we realize that it is, in essence, an internal issue between God and us, then we can begin to take the steps necessary to release the controller from his actions. As we are able to do that, we keep our hearts clear from bitterness and anger.

In order to experience the power of true forgiveness, we must also determine our values. In other words, forgiveness requires that we place *more value* on what Jesus accomplished on the cross through His finished work than we do on the wrongdoing of others. Our refusal to forgive and to genuinely love the abuser is often an attempt to punish the one who has hurt us.

When we have been hurt, our natural instincts—our carnality—often want to see the offender receive the same abuse that he or she inflicted on us. We want to see them "get theirs," so to speak. Our anger toward them is our attempt to regain a sense of control, as well as to punish them for their wrongs. When this is our response, we have taken the place of God.

The issue of forgiveness has nothing to do with the offender. It is an internal issue between God and us.

Within all of us, there is an inner sense of justice. Instinctively we need to see inequities righted and the scales of justice balanced. When we have been hurt or abused, the scales in our hearts become dramatically tipped in the direction of injustice. We realize the imbalance must be resolved. Unforgiveness is our attempt to bring the scales back to a place of balance— to right the wrong.

145

But we are valuing the wrong thing. Each day that we hold on to the hurt, anger and bitterness, we are placing more value on the offense than on the blood of Jesus. The only way to experience true forgiveness and to balance the scales of injustice is to place more value on what Jesus did *for* us than on what others have done *to* us.

In Ephesians 4:32 we read, "And be kind to one another, tenderhearted, forgiving one another, even as God in Christ forgave you." When reading this verse we need to remind ourselves of how God, in Christ, has forgiven us. God forgave us long before we had enough sense to ask for His forgiveness. Therefore, if you are waiting for the controller to come to his senses and ask for your forgiveness before you forgive him, you will probably live many years in bitterness and anger.

The last part of the verse says, "Even as God in Christ forgave *you.*" Think about it, God has forgiven you! You didn't deserve His love or forgiveness. In other words, if God has forgiven us when we didn't deserve it, what right do we have to hold another man's sin against Him?

2. SPEAK WITH YOUR PASTOR OR SOMEONE IN LEADERSHIP ABOUT YOUR CONCERNS.

Make sure you don't get trapped into speaking to everyone else about your feelings concerning the church. Talk with your pastor or someone in leadership about your concerns. Give the pastor a chance to respond. Two things are possible: It may be that what you interpreted as a spirit of control may, in fact, have been genuine concern for your welfare. If that is true, it gives you an opportunity to make an adjustment in your own heart. Second, if the pastor is indeed operating in a spirit of control, honest and loving confrontation may result in your pastor's making an adjustment in his heart and breaking free from that controlling spirit.

When speaking with your pastor or church leader, be sure to stay in a humble attitude. Refrain from saying anything unkind or critical. Prepare your mind and heart before you go to speak with him. What we say is often less important than how we say it. Be sure to win the battle of frustration and anger privately first. As you establish your heart in the love of God, you will be able to get your motives right and gain perspective and control. As you draw from the resource of God's love, you will be able to refrain from speaking impulsively or from striking out in anger.

Don't forget the power of your words. Words have the power to heal or to injure, and they have the ability to ignite strife or to stop it.

> A soft answer turns away wrath, but a harsh word stirs up anger. The tongue of the wise uses knowledge rightly, but the mouth of fools pours forth foolishness.
>
> —PROVERBS 15:1–2

It is clear that what we say creates a spiritual climate. Therefore, we can create a climate that is conducive for healing and restoration, or we can create a climate for division and strife. More than likely you have an opportunity to use your words to illicit love and tenderness in the hearts of people—or to create judgment and criticism.

3. DISTINGUISH BETWEEN THE ABUSER AND HIS OR HER ACTIONS.

Even though we disagree passionately with the acts of control, at the same time we must recognize the intrinsic worth of each person—even of the controlling leader. In order to guard our hearts from judgment, we must be able to accept that a person has worth simply because God loves that person. In the same way that God loves us despite our actions, we too must recognize the love and value God places on others despite their actions.

Nothing reinforces a controlling attitude more than judgment. When a person begins to feel acceptance and worth, it frees that person from the need to defend himself or herself.

147

When we accept a person, it does not mean that we are condoning that person's behavior or agreeing with his or her opinion. By no means does accepting a controlling leader mean that we are excusing that leader's

Each day that we hold on to the hurt, anger and bitterness, we are placing more value on the offense than on the blood of Jesus.

abuse. Acceptance simply keeps us from sitting in the seat of the judge, and it enables us to remain in the place of the intercessor. The only way you will ever be able to forgive and love the controlling leader is to separate their worth from their sins.

It is important to learn this truth: Long after you have gone from an abusive situation, you need to be able to keep your heart tender toward the pastor of that abusive church.

4. EXERCISE PATIENCE.

As you leave an unhealthy church, many times you will find yourself in a whirlwind of false accusations. Often the very people you thought would never turn against you—do. This is the time to exercise patience before God and toward others. I have heard it said that patience is the practical expression of faith, hope, wisdom and love.

Patience is an active emotion. It is not passive or resigned to defeat. Patience is emotional diligence. It involves the ability to carry the weight of disappointment, while trusting God for the outcome. Patience is a mark of maturity and a fruit of love. It demonstrates that we care more about someone else's welfare than our own. James 1:4 gives us some good advice:

> But let patience have its perfect work, that you may be perfect and complete, lacking nothing.

The word *perfect* is the Greek word *teleios*. Literally, it means to be a full-grown adult as opposed to a little child. It denotes two separate ideas. One alludes to the biological growth process from infancy to adulthood and illustrates that we go through the same process as we grow spiritually. Exhibiting patience during times of adversity and hardship is the mark of mature spiritual adulthood. The Greek word also alludes to the growth process in the womb from the time a baby is conceived to the point of birth. This latter concept is what caused the translators of the King James Version to use the word *her*, causing the text to read, "But let patience have *her* perfect work, that ye may be perfect [mature] and entire [complete], wanting nothing."

149

Just as it is essential for a woman to endure the discomfort of the nine-month gestation period before her child is born, so we must endure patiently in the discomforts and even pain that our trials may bring us. If we do, then we are fully developed as Christians.

In Psalm 31:15 we read, "My times are in Your hand; deliver me from the hands of my enemies, and from those who persecute me." God is the One who defends. If we take matters into our own hands and try to defend ourselves, then we tie God's hands from being able to defend us.

Who would you rather come to your defense?

5. Don't get caught up in arguments and disputes.

You will have plenty of opportunities to get into a war of words with others. Don't feel that you have to answer irresponsible accusations. If you try to answer or argue, you will probably stir up additional hostility and drain your own spiritual and emotional energy. In Proverbs 26:4 we read, "Do not answer a fool according to his folly, lest you also be like him." Proverbs 29:11 expands that thought by adding, "A fool vents all his feelings, but a wise man holds them back."

Trust the Lord to be your shield. Determine to find your worth and security in His love for you—not in the words or attitudes of others. The more you see your worth through God's love, the more worth you will have in your emotional bank account. When your emotional account is full because you have discovered your value in His love, then you will feel that you can afford to "write a check" of forgiveness and kindness.

6. Live the law of love.

I believe that it is important not to give up on people. Our tendency is to think that if we have been patient with someone for a long time, and that person still haven't changed, then we have the justification to write that relationship off. We often call it "tough love." There are times when love must be tough. There are times when we can't continue to rescue people and protect them from the consequences of their decisions. Yet, at the same time, we can't afford to throw in the towel and lose faith that the person will ever change.

The abusive leader is controlling because of his deep sense of insecurity. He hasn't discovered His worth in God's love. He acts tough and hard in an attempt to hide the very fears and insecurities that

150

drive him and bring abuse to his relationships. Underneath, he really is frightened. He is frightened that the very ones he desires to impress are the ones who will reject him. Because he believes he needs the acceptance of others to be someone of worth, he will fight desperately for everyone's approval.

If he is ever going to be free, he needs to experience love and not judgment. If we will listen with our third ear—our heart—we will be able to hear his fears within his words. As we show love, many of these controllers will experience for the first time the love of God in a tangible way.

7. Don't give up or give in.

If after speaking with your pastor or church leader, enlisting the wise counsel of objective, mature people and checking your heart and attitude you know that you are in an unhealthy church, you are free to go. But before you go, you must be absolutely convinced that you are doing the right thing before God. There are consequences to any decision you make in life. If you are in an abusive church, there are severe long-range consequences to staying in that situation. In the same way, if you choose to leave, there will also be consequences. Your convictions are the only thing that will carry you through the consequences. Even if you know inwardly that you should leave, if you lack the conviction to do so, your fear of the consequences will keep you imprisoned in that unhealthy environment.

You can't be concerned about hurting your pastor's feelings. It is unfair to shield people from the consequences of their behavior. If we do, then we are empowering them in a direction that is destructive. If we continue to attend an abusive church for fear of the

151

leader's feelings, then we foster a law-unto-themselves attitude. We never do someone a favor by taking the path of least resistance.

One of the biggest mistakes we make is attempting to build or rebuild a relationship without any change in the conduct or attitude that was abusive and destructive. There are fundamental, foundational truths upon which any relationship must be founded for that relationship to be healthy. These foundational truths apply not only for interpersonal relationships, but also relationships with spiritual leaders.

A controlling leader consistently believes that in order for any relationship with him to be maintained, it must be completely on his terms. He must be in charge of every aspect of the relationship.

Often it is painful to allow the controller to sever the relationship through his actions. Even if we have distanced ourselves, when we are around the abusive leader we may be tempted to take an inordinately submissive role. We may think that by doing so we have navigated around the leader's insecurities, when in fact we have merely fed them.

If we respond in that way, we probably think we have been able to maintain our relationship with that leader. In actuality, the friendship isn't real—it is fundamentally marked with inconsistency and insincerity. At that point it doesn't matter how many "relationship" techniques you use. Holding on to long-term relationships isn't always a sign of spiritual maturity—not if the relationship is cemented in deception and control. The idea of maintaining long-term relationships cannot supercede truth.

In the year 2000 there were several high-profile pastors and preachers in the Charismatic ranks who became involved in adultery. Many of them vehemently denied involvement with other women, yet they were remarried before the ink was dry on their divorce papers. The people who continue to fill their sanctuaries or come to their meetings are doing these

There are fundamental, foundational truths upon which any relationship must be founded for that relationship to be healthy.

men a great disservice. The high-profile preachers who come to preach in the pulpits of these morally fallen pastors are doing these men and the entire body of Christ a disservice. By not allowing these men to take responsibility for their actions, they are keeping them in a place of weakness and spiritually crippling them for the rest of their lives. We are also teaching the body of Christ that personality, image, talent, charisma and charm are more important than integrity. Don't buy the lie that you are obligated to follow a man who lacks integrity and moral fiber just because he holds the title of a "pastor."

153

8. DON'T CREATE A CRISIS TO JUSTIFY YOUR DECISION TO LEAVE.

Many times when we are unhappy or frustrated in a church we will create a crisis by doing or saying something that forces the pastor's hand. In essence we are picking a fight so that we have another excuse to leave.

Remember, the way you walk out one door will determine the way you enter the next door.

9. DON'T HOLD OR PARTICIPATE IN SECRET MEETINGS ABOUT THE CHURCH OR PASTOR.

Many times this is done in the guise of "praying for the pastor." Meetings like these are always a seedbed for a critical and judgmental spirit. No matter how ungodly your pastor is, no one has a right to begin to section off the body and hold secret meetings to discuss how bad things are. Again, if you are that convinced that things are not right, then simply leave.

It is not your responsibility to try to rescue your friends. If they come to you with questions, answer their questions. But then you must refer them to the Scriptures and encourage them to go through the same process as you, which involves first speaking with the pastor or church leader. But don't make overt attempts to influence others to leave the church. If they leave, it must be their decision, based on what the Lord has shown them.

154

If you influence others to leave, then they will lack the conviction necessary to follow through. Because it was your influence, and not the result of their own convictions, they may find it difficult to guard their hearts from bitterness or to search out a healthy church to attend.

As you go through the process of leaving an abusive church, you may feel that you can never trust another pastor again. You may feel safer staying at home on Sundays. You may be tempted to give up on church altogether. Though this time may be difficult, life is not over. Your future is not over.

I challenge you not to give in to the feelings of desperation or hopelessness. Press into your relationship with Jesus. Don't become "missing in action" concerning being a part of a local church. God loves you. In Luke 4:18 Jesus said:

> The Spirit of the LORD is upon Me, because He has anointed Me to preach the gospel to the poor; He has sent Me to heal the brokenhearted; to proclaim liberty to the captives and recovery of sight to the blind, to set at liberty those who are oppressed.

The way you walk out one door will determine the way you enter the next door.

Those words are as true today as they were two thousand years ago. Jesus is still anointed to bind up the brokenhearted. He is here to bind up your broken heart today. Let Him. As you do, you will experience His freedom.

155

QUESTIONS

Chapter 7
Breaking Ties With the Abusive System

1. Sadly, many Christians who leave abusive churches are "cursed" or shunned by their former pastor and other church members. How do you think a person should respond if he or she is treated in this way?

_____

_____

_____

_____

_____

_____

_____

2. Why is it so important that we guard our hearts from unforgiveness if we have been in an abusive church situation?

_____

_____

_____

_____

_____

_____

_____

_____

3. Have you ever had to leave a church because of problems with the pastor? Describe the situation and how you felt.

_____

_____

_____

_____

_____

_____

4. Why is it so important to love the abusive leader regardless of what he or she did to you?

_____

_____

_____

_____

_____

_____

5. How can a person who leaves an abusive church gain the ability to trust a pastor again?

_____

_____

_____

_____

_____

_____

CHAPTER 8

GOD
HAS A HEALTHY
CHURCH FOR YOU

BLESSING:
NO SPIRITUAL ABUSE AHEAD

"I will set up shepherds over them who will feed them; and they shall fear no more, nor be dismayed, nor shall they be lacking," says the LORD.

—JEREMIAH 23:4

The most tragic result of unhealthy and abusive churches is the thousands of Christians who give up on the church altogether. When the church has hurt us, we can have the tendency to do what the old adage says—to "throw the baby out with the bath water." Many people who have been wounded by an abusive spiritual leader decide to avoid involvement in the church or even attending a local church. Many who have been hurt by the church conclude that the very idea of a "local church" is the problem. Such a mind-set can lead to worldly philosophies that declare the local church is the invention of man and that God never intended for the local church to exist.

The local church is not the problem behind spiritual abuse. In actuality, the local church has always been in the heart and mind of God. From the birth of the church in the second chapter of the Book of Acts, it has been clear that God's intent is for the local church to be the vehicle that drives the message of the gospel around the world.

Each of the epistles written by the apostle Paul was written as a letter that was addressed to a specific church in one of the cities where he had preached. When Paul arrived in an area or city, immediately he would establish a group of elders, along with a pastor, to lead that particular congregation. The Book of 1 Timothy is a letter written by the apostle Paul to Timothy. Timothy was a part of Paul's apostolic team, and he was involved in ministry with Paul in the cities of Thessalonica, Macedonia, Jerusalem and Corinth. At some point in time, Paul left Timothy in Ephesus, yet the local church was so important to Paul that he took time to write to Timothy and give him instructions about how the local church is to operate. First

161

Timothy is one of the most exhaustive instructions in the Bible concerning the function of the local church.

The church is not a building— the church is those who collectively and individually have heard and answered Jesus' call.

As one example, Paul instructed Timothy to deal directly with false teachers who crept into the church in Ephesus, telling Timothy:

> As I urged you when I went into Macedonia— remain in Ephesus that you may charge some that they teach no other doctrine, nor give heed to fables and endless genealogies, which cause disputes rather than godly edification which is in faith.
>
> —1 TIMOTHY 1:3–4

162

Paul's letter to Timothy also instructed him regarding the elements necessary in a corporate worship service:

> Therefore I exhort first of all that supplications, prayers, intercessions, and giving of thanks be made for all men, for kings and all who are in authority, that we may lead a quiet and peaceable life in all godliness and reverence. For this is good and acceptable in the sight of God our Savior.
>
> —1 TIMOTHY 2:1–3

In his same letter, the apostle Paul gave detailed

instructions concerning the selection of elders and deacons, as well as how they are to function in the local church. Paul's instructions were very specific—even to explaining how the local church was to treat widows and orphans as well as tackling the controversial question of a woman's role in the church.

The remainder of Paul's epistles—as well as many portions throughout the New Testament—clearly teach us that the role of the local church is God's idea.

THE CHURCH IS SUPERNATURAL

Webster defines *church* as "a building for public, especially Christian, worship." God's definition of the church is radically different. In Matthew 16:18 Jesus spoke of the church, saying, "And I also say to you that you are Peter, and on this rock I will build My church, and the gates of Hades shall not prevail against it." The word *church* in this verse is the Greek word *ekklesia*, which literally means "called-out ones." This word is used by Jesus to describe those who are His followers.

163

The church is not a building—the church is those who collectively and individually have heard and answered Jesus' call. The very definition of the word *church* implies the initiating voice of God—He is the one who has called us. He is the one who initiated the work of salvation. God pursued us. He called out to us with the message of hope and redemption. Those who had ears to hear responded to His voice and received His salvation. The church, therefore, truly was God's idea, initiated by His voice calling us out of the world and unto to Himself.

Yet, we are not only called to Jesus, but we are also called to one another.

> For by one Spirit we were all baptized into one body—whether Jews or Greeks, whether slaves or free—and have all been made to drink into one Spirit. For in fact the body is not one member but many.
>
> —1 Corinthians 12:13–14

It is certainly true that individually each of us is His church. But collectively we are also His church and His body. It is clear that, just as we are called into relationship with Christ, we are also called into relationship with one another. One of the most tragic consequences of spiritual abuse is that it fragments the body of Christ. Once abuse has taken place, our relationships within the church become poisoned. Fear replaces confidence, suspicion replaces trust, and insecurity replaces servanthood.

The Marks of a Healthy Church

Since we are His church and therefore called to one another, and since the local church is God's will for us, we are faced with the opportunity to connect with a local body of believers. Yet, if we have already left one church because of spiritual abuse, the last thing we want to do is find ourselves once again in an unhealthy and abusive situation. In looking for a church, there are some questions we need to ask ourselves: "What are the characteristics of a healthy church?" "What should I look for in a church?" "What should I expect from a healthy church?"

There is a difference between a healthy church and the perfect church. Very simply put, the difference is this—the perfect church doesn't exist! Let's take a look, then, at five marks of a healthy church.

164

1. The healthy church understands its purpose.

In Philippians 3:10 we read, "That I may know Him and the power of His resurrection, and the fellowship of His sufferings, being conformed to His death." This was the heart cry of the apostle Paul! Not only is Paul expressing the deepest desire of his heart, but also in the words of this verse we discover the main purpose we have as the church. The Amplified Version sheds additional light on what Paul is saying:

> [For my determined purpose is] that I may know Him [that I may progressively become more deeply and intimately acquainted with Him, perceiving and recognizing and understanding the wonders of His Person more strongly and clearly], and that I may in that same way come to know the power outflowing from His resurrection [which it exerts over believers], and that I may so share His sufferings as to be continually transformed [in spirit into His likeness even] to His death.
> —Philippians 3:10, AMP

165

Paul understood that his ultimate purpose was to know Christ. This "knowing" of Christ isn't referring to a greater knowledge *about* Christ. It means experiencing Him on a deeper and more intimate level.

The perfect church doesn't exist!

In Mark 3:13–15 we read the account of Jesus' selecting the twelve disciples:

And He went up on the mountain and called to Him those He Himself wanted. And they came to Him. Then He appointed twelve, that they might be with Him and that He might send them out to preach, and to have power to heal sicknesses and to cast out demons.

The purpose of the church is to draw people into a personal relationship with Christ.

Notice the first appointment the Twelve had was to *be with Him*. The disciples' primary calling was to have relationship with Jesus. God didn't redeem us because He wanted more employees. He redeemed us to restore the relationship with man that had been lost through sin.

We also see in this passage that the disciples' secondary calling was to preach the gospel and to heal the sick. Not only are we called to relationship with Christ, but we are also called to be His expression of life, love and power here on the earth. The Amplified translation of Ephesians 1:23 reads:

166

Which is His body, the fullness of Him Who fills all in all [for in that body lives the full measure of Him Who makes everything complete, and who fills everything everywhere with Himself].

According to this scripture, the full measure of Christ lives within us, His body. In addition, it is within (and through) the church—His body—that God literally fills everything everywhere with the reality of who Christ is! A healthy church understands that its primary purpose is to bring people into a personal and progressively more intimate relationship with Jesus. A healthy church also understands its responsibility to demonstrate to the world the reality of our relationship with Christ in a tangible way.

The purpose of the church is not to become well known or for the pastor to become famous. The purpose of the church is to draw people into a personal relationship with Christ. When the church loses sight of its primary purpose, then the mechanics of organization become more important than people. If that happens, people begin to be viewed as a resource necessary to serve the organization, instead of viewing the church's purpose as being there to serve the people.

2. WITHIN A HEALTHY CHURCH THE GROUND IS LEVEL.
In 1 Corinthians 12:13–14 we read:

> For by one Spirit we were all baptized into one body—whether Jews or Greeks, whether slaves or free—and have all been made to drink into one Spirit. For in fact the body is not one member but many.

167

Notice that Paul says "whether Jews or Greeks... slaves or free." The Scripture is saying that the church should be void of *any* form of prejudice. The phrase "whether Jews or Greeks" speaks of racial prejudice. We, as Christ's body, are bonded together by more than shared values and ideologies. We as the church are bonded together by the blood of Jesus. His Spirit seals us to Christ and to one another. In the kingdom of God the color of a man's skin doesn't determine his value or worth.

The Book of Revelation gives us a beautiful picture of heaven and shows us how God views His church:

> After these things I looked, and behold, a great multitude which no one could number, of all nations, tribes, peoples, and tongues, standing before the throne and before the Lamb, clothed with white robes, with palm branches in their hands.
>
> —REVELATION 7:9

The church—both here and in heaven—should include "all nations, tribes, peoples, and tongues"!

The phrase "slaves or free" in 1 Corinthians 12:13 addresses social prejudice. Just as the color of a man's skin doesn't determine his worth, neither does a man's social standing determine his worth in the kingdom of God. A man's financial status determines his standing or position in society—not in Christ's church. The Book of James speaks directly to partiality shown in the church toward those who have financial means:

168

> My brethren, do not hold the faith of our Lord Jesus Christ, the Lord of glory, with partiality. For if there should come into your assembly a man with gold rings, in fine apparel, and there should also come in a poor man in filthy clothes, and you pay attention to the one wearing the fine clothes and say to him, "You sit here in a good place," and say to the poor man, "You stand there," or, "Sit here at my footstool," have you not shown partiality among yourselves, and become judges with evil thoughts?
>
> —JAMES 2:1–4

A healthy church refuses to show any partiality

based on a man's income. We should avoid prejudice toward the poor or the rich. In other words, we cannot afford to place more or less value on an individual based on that person's financial status. We should neither judge the poor for being poor, nor the rich for being rich.

3. A HEALTHY CHURCH IS A CHURCH OF WORSHIP.

In Matthew 4 we read of Jesus' being tempted by Satan. At the conclusion of a forty-day fast, Jesus was approached by Satan, who attempted to deceive Jesus in three areas. One of the areas was regarding worship.

> Again, the devil took Him up on an exceedingly high mountain, and showed Him all the kingdoms of the world and their glory. And he said to Him, "All these things I will give You if You will fall down and worship me."
>
> —MATTHEW 4:8–9

It is clear that Satan is seeking to pervert the area of worship in the life of Christ. The word *worship* is the Greek word *proskuneo*. It is from this word that we derive our English word *prostrate*, which means to assume the posture of lying flat before someone in an attitude of total surrender.

169

All the power of the world was promised to Jesus if He would only surrender Himself to Satan. It is important to remember that all the powers of the world had previously belonged to Jesus. He relinquished those powers by becoming man. Jesus operated in power, but He did so by virtue of His relationship with the Father. One day Jesus would win those powers back, but it would only be accomplished through the extreme sacrifice of the cross.

Satan was promising Jesus an easier way. He was promising Jesus the return of all authority without the pain of the cross. All Jesus had to do was bow down to him and worship him.

It is possible to become so involved in serving that we do so at the expense of our relationship with Jesus.

In Matthew 4:10 we read Jesus' response:

> Then Jesus said to him, "Away with you, Satan! For it is written, 'You shall worship the LORD your God, and Him only you shall serve.'"

Satan may offer an easier way to what may seem like a life of abundance. But there is no other way to a life of abundance and power—except through true worship of the Lord. A healthy church exalts the lordship of Christ in every area of life in that church. A healthy church desires to produce disciples of Jesus—not disciples of men.

This verse in Matthew shares another important message—that of the priority of worship and service to God. Jesus said, "You shall worship the LORD your God, and Him only you shall serve." The worship *of* God comes before service *to* God.

In an unhealthy church, our commitment to God is often measured by how busy we are in serving the church. In an unhealthy church it is implied that the only way truly to serve God is by serving the church. Please don't misunderstand my point—serving

170

actively in the church is indeed a way of serving God and the kingdom. But it is not the only way.

It is possible to become so involved in serving that we do so at the expense of our relationship with Jesus. Servanthood is certainly a cornerstone for being a disciple of Jesus. But we must watch that we don't reverse the divine order. Our service must be a by-product of our worship.

In unhealthy churches, one's love for God is often defined by the individual's involvement in the activities of the church. But in a healthy church, members are encouraged to worship the Lord *first.* Then—and only then—should we serve Him.

4. A HEALTHY CHURCH IS A CHURCH THAT SERVES PEOPLE.

Our service should be an outflow of our worship. Those who truly worship the Father automatically live a life of servanthood. At one point the Pharisees asked Jesus to tell them the greatest commandment of the Law. Jesus responded by saying:

> "You shall love the LORD your God with all your heart, with all your soul, and with all your mind." This is the first and great commandment. And the second is like it: *"You shall love your neighbor as yourself."*
> —MATTHEW 22:37–39, EMPHASIS ADDED

171

In a healthy church, faithfulness often is defined by more than just church attendance. Though church attendance is important, it is not a true indication of servanthood or faithfulness. True faithfulness is demonstrated by our willingness to serve others. In Ephesians 4:12 we read, "...for the equipping of the saints for the work of the ministry, for the edifying of the body of Christ." The word *edifying* is the Greek word *oikodome*, which is defined as "to build up." It can also be translated as "the act of building." It conveys the meaning that as each member of the body of Christ serves one another, the result is that the entire body is being fashioned and strengthened in the power of God.

God designed His body to function together. It is only as each member serves the other that the body of Christ is able to function in her ultimate potential.

A healthy church is one that has her eyes on the harvest.

In 1 Corinthians 12:5 we read, "There are differences of ministries, but the same Lord." The word *differences* is the Greek word *diairesis*. The meaning of this word involves the dividing or distribution of various gifts. Paul is referring to the different gifts or abilities that God has given to each one in the body of Christ.

172 God has given each one certain gifts or abilities. These gifts have been strategically distributed to every member by the will of God. As we choose to serve each other with these gifts, together we experience a power and grace that we would never discover on our own.

In 1 Corinthians 12:5 we also see the word *ministries*, which is *diakonia* in the Greek. This word comes from the Greek word *diakoneo*, which means "to serve," as a slave would serve his master. The word *diakonia* involves service that results from a compassionate love toward the needy in the Christian community. A healthy church is a church full of compassion that results in an attitude of service.

The Bible helps us to understand how to serve

through the words of Jesus in Mark 10:42–43, where we read:

> But Jesus called them to Himself and said to them, "You know that those who are considered rulers over the Gentiles lord it over them, and their great ones exercise authority over them. Yet it shall not be so among you; but whoever desires to become great among you shall be your servant."

Jesus was saying that the measure of our lives is not determined by the position we attain in life, but rather by the sacrifices we make. In a later verse, Jesus said, "For even the Son of Man did not come to be served, but to serve, and to give His life a ransom for many" (v. 45).

5. A HEALTHY CHURCH IS A CHURCH THAT REACHES PEOPLE. Jesus gave every believer the same instructions:

> Go therefore and make disciples of all the nations, baptizing them in the name of the Father and of the Son and of the Holy Spirit, teaching them to observe all things that I have commanded you; and lo, I am with you always, even to the end of the age.
>
> —MATTHEW 28:19–20

173

A healthy church is one that has her eyes on the harvest. As long as there are those who don't know Christ in our communities, we must continue to discover innovative ways to reach them with the gospel. It is when we lose our vision for the lost that we begin to become self-absorbed. When we believe the church's purpose is simply to come together once or twice a week to hear the Word, eventually we become overly introspective. Often this results in the body beginning to turn on itself with a spirit of criticism and strife. I like to say it this way: "If we sit and soak too long, and don't do—then eventually we sour!" It is difficult to be critical of one another if we are standing shoulder to shoulder to reach the lost.

God has a church for you where love replaces fear, a church where hope replaces dismay, and a church where abundance replaces lack.

Each of these five characteristics is essential in a healthy, life-giving church. Yet, the emphasis must be evenly distributed among the five. Some churches make the mistake of placing more emphasis on one characteristic over the others. For example, some churches have such an emphasis on evangelism that they neglect the needs of the existing families in their church. In a church with a strong evangelistic thrust, those who aren't involved in soulwinning often are made to feel guilty and are accused of not being compassionate toward the lost.

In the same way, it is possible to overemphasize discipleship or prayer or worship. All of these aspects of church life are necessary. But we cannot afford to stress one over the other. To do so, in and of itself, is not abusive, but it can certainly make room for future abuse to take place. It is a constant challenge for a church to maintain these five characteristics.

A tragic mistake some believers make is allowing past abuse to keep them from being a part of a local church.

If you have been abused in one church, it would be a very easy thing to isolate yourself from a local body for fear of being hurt again. Yet, as we have seen, it is God's will to be an active part of a healthy church.

Allow me to make a statement that might help you be willing to take the risk of being a part of a healthy local church: I believe a healthy church is off track about 80 percent of the time. That may initially seem like a bizarre statement. You may ask, "Mike, if a healthy church is indeed off track about 80 percent of the time, then what makes it healthy?"

Allow me to explain further. A healthy church knows when it is off track and is willing to make the necessary course corrections to get "back on track" fulfilling its purpose and mission. Therefore, as soon as it realizes that it needs to make a course correction, it does so. Making those necessary corrections 80 percent of the time equals a healthy church—but failing to make course corrections can lead quickly to an unhealthy church environment.

There are far more healthy churches out there than there are unhealthy churches. There are churches all over this country that are led by honest pastors who love God with all their hearts. In my travels I have been encouraged to see that most pastors simply want to build God's kingdom, love the people and lead them to a strong relationship with Jesus. Unfortunately, the pastors who have had ulterior motives have left thousands of wounded believers in the wake of their steamboat ambitions.

You may be one of those. I want you to know that Jesus is still anointed to heal the brokenhearted. I pray that these words of the prophet Jeremiah bring you hope and comfort:

"I will set up shepherds over them who will feed them; and they shall fear no more, nor be dismayed, nor shall they be lacking," says the LORD.
—JEREMIAH 23:4

This is God's promise for you. God has a shepherd for you and your family. I want to challenge you to receive this promise. Expect Jesus to lead you to the church He has for you. Pray and ask Him where you need to go. Begin to visit the churches in your area, and trust Christ to lead you. God has a church for you where love replaces fear, a church where hope replaces dismay and a church where abundance replaces lack.

176

Chapter 8
God Has a Healthy Church for You

1. When people experience spiritual abuse in a church, they are often tempted to reject church altogether. Sometimes they also become bitter. How do you think these unhealthy reactions can be avoided?

_____

_____

_____

_____

_____

_____

_____

_____

2. We are sometimes tempted to equate service to God with service to the local church. Explain why this is dangerous.

_____

_____

_____

_____

_____

_____

_____

_____

3. Based on the five characteristics of a healthy church listed in this chapter, in what areas do you feel your church needs to improve?

_____

_____

_____

_____

_____

_____

_____

_____

4. How can you personally be used by God to make positive changes in your local church?

_____

_____

_____

_____

_____

_____

_____

_____